Dedication

Dedicated to the family of Harry and Helen Waggoner and to Doree Donaldson—the granddaughter of this beloved missionary couple and the wife of Hal Donaldson.

Contents

Forewords

For many years, missionary Harry Waggoner carried on a God-blessed ministry among a class of very needy people —lepers in northern India. He ministered to their physical needs and shared the message of God's saving grace to meet their spiritual needs.

Upon his retirement from missionary endeavors overseas, Brother Waggoner engaged in ministry in the homeland. For a period of time he was the pastor of my home church, where my father was on the deacon board from the founding of the church until his death. During Brother Waggoner's pastoral ministry, they developed a warm and enduring friendship. The name Harry Waggoner was often recalled with great fondness and esteem.

The lifetime of service to India's downtrodden by this selfless servant of God deserves the highest respect and honor.

G. Raymond Carlson
General Superintendent
Assemblies of God

I am grateful for the opportunity to write a foreword for this book on Harry Waggoner. His life represented the pioneer work of missionaries in India.

More than thirty-six years ago, when my husband and I came to Calcutta, we saw the labors of those who had spent forty and fifty years in this country. Our hearts were touched by their dedication and love for the people of this needy land.

Scripture is so true: "One soweth and another reapeth . . . but God gave the increase" (John 4:37, 1 Corinthians 3:6). Today, in India, we are indeed reaping what was sown in the sacrificial lives and prayers of so many faithful ambassadors of missions before us.

This is a new day in India—a new generation with changing customs and cultures. Nevertheless, we know that the laborers who preceded us worked under adverse circumstances in remote areas so we might have the heritage of the Assemblies of God mission in India. Their lives, love, and encouragement helped us in the early days to press on to fulfill God's plan; for this we are grateful.

I am, therefore, glad that one of these faithful pioneers has been honored in this book. I would like to add my admiration and love for its authors—my nephew Kenneth M. Dobson and Hal Donaldson—and express my gratitude to all the pioneers of the Assemblies of God mission who preceded us in this great land.

Huldah Buntain
Missionary, India

Among my most pleasant memories is the relationship between my father, A. G. Ward, and Harry Waggoner. The Reverend Waggoner had grown up in Warren, Ohio, near where my parents were pastoring in New Castle, Pennsylvania. A kinship of spirit was immediate.

The burden for India's outcast, especially the misery of lepers, had fastened upon Brother Waggoner. He felt a compulsion to do something about it. He shared the burden with my parents. The Spirit of God brought them into an accord, and immediately pointed the direction for the Waggoners' return to India and the need for my parents to do all within their power to advance the mission and raise the support.

Many times I was involved in the mailings and distribution of literature and appeals for funding. It was truly a faith mission. God blessed it from the beginning, however, and Harry Waggoner gave a lifetime of service to the lepers. His name and testimony deserve the highest respect. He with his family were selfless workers and became forerunners to many leprosariums within the nation. I retain the fondest memories of those days of faith and advancement.

Dr. C. M. Ward
Author, Evangelist

Acknowledgments

Special recognition to the family of Harry Waggoner, Debra Petrosky, Matt Key, and Joe Johnston for their contribution to this project.

My deepest appreciation goes to my wife, Kathy, who is my best friend and partner in ministry; to my children Brooke, Brittany, and Bobby, who are constant sources of joy; and to my mother, Beulah Dobson, for her ongoing support.

Heartfelt thanks to Dale Neill, Tony Gage, Skip Spohn, and Nolan Green, and Bob Schueller, members of the church board at Paramount, First Assembly of God. They encouraged me to write. I am also indebted to the following who helped to make this project possible: Lionel Madafford, Dr. Huldah Buntain, Ken McElhoes, Dr. Gerry Roberts, and Ken Roberts.

Kenneth M. Dobson

Introduction

I never had the privilege of meeting Harry Waggoner. In fact, I was only six years old in 1963 when his wife, children, and grandchildren gathered around his casket in Caldwell, Idaho. Twenty-five years later, however, whether by chance or divine providence, the life of this obscure missionary captured my curiosity. And, after months of deliberation, I decided an account of his life was indeed worthy of being told.

Kenneth M. Dobson and I set out to learn as much as we could about this man who gave his life for the lepers of India. As his friends and family corroborated stories of his compassion and the selfless lifestyle he led, the more vivid our mental images became. I could almost see him wiping his brow as he endeavored to build a home for lepers, shoveling dirt and stacking bricks under the sun's stinging rays. I could visualize him foregoing a meal so a hungry beggar would have something to eat. I could envision him feeding goat milk to an infant orphan.

The legacy of Harry Waggoner spun into shape as we collected one stirring anecdote after another. We heard a myriad of stories that provided glimpses of his faith and doubt, accomplishments and failures, joys and sorrows. Finally, after months of research, we felt as though we "knew" Harry Waggoner and thus could begin writing his biography.

From the outset, we were bent on penning an idolizing portrait of an unheralded man who embodied self-denial and compassion, one who could serve as a model for "successful" Christian living. But before the first chapter was completed, we realized there was little eternal value in enshrining Harry Waggoner. And if he were living, he too would have objected to that notion. Perhaps the message to be gleaned from Harry Waggoner's life is more aptly a testimony of his Creator's mercy—a God who so desired to offer hope to the despised and neglected of India that He escorted a country boy to a jungle halfway around the globe. That was the real story; for there, God's servant—Harry Waggoner—became known throughout the countryside as "the friend of lepers."

The Vow is a reminder of the valor of obedient sacrifice—the honor found in doing God's will regardless of the consequences.

One story, in particular, illustrates Harry Waggoner's obedience to God even though it meant placing his own life in jeopardy. It was after midnight when Harry and his wife Helen were awakened by a loud but muffled moan approaching their sleeping quarters. At first it sounded like a rabid animal that had wandered near their bungalow. The noise intensified before Harry's cocked ear recognized it as the cry of a man in torment.

Harry crawled from under his mosquito net, his body sticky with perspiration. Accompanied by a lantern, he stepped into the stillness of the night with the eery impression that someone was watching.

Suddenly, a voice screamed, "Sahib, Sahib!"

Harry's head rotated in the direction of the gasping plea. "Sahib!"

In his bare feet, Harry scurried to the base of a mango tree where the despairing man had fallen.

"Sahib, I am being eaten alive by worms. I am a leper and in great misery. They told me you would help me."

"Don't worry, we will help you," Harry said, lowering the lantern to inspect the man's ailment. The leper lifted his loin cloth, unveiling a huge festering sore, maggots literally feasting on the man's flesh. Years earlier, such a sight would have wrenched Harry's stomach, but now that he had become numb to the ugliness, it merely brought tears to his eyes. He knew Jesus wanted him to aid the man despite the obvious danger of contracting the disease himself.

The missionary stood. "I will return. Stay here."

"Sahib, help me!" the man cried at Harry's back. "Do not leave me to die."

Moments later, Harry returned with tweezers and a bowl of disinfectant, and, undauntedly, began removing the worms and cleansing the sordid wound.

The leper was silent, pondering this white man's disregard for his own safety. How the missionary differed from the leper's family and village who had banished him forever and marked him as "unclean." Never had he witnessed such a display of sacrificial love.

Once a bandage was in place, the leper nearly awakened the entire community offering hearty "salaams" to his rescuer. "Thank you, thank you, thank you, Sahib!" he yelled time and again, clasping his hands together on his forehead and bowing his face to the ground.

It was some weeks later that the leper accepted Christ as his personal Savior.

Many lepers found Jesus over the years—largely because one missionary stayed true to the vow he made as a youth: to obey his Master's voice regardless of the cost. When Jesus walked the earth, He touched lepers and made them whole. Through Harry Waggoner's life, Jesus continued to touch lepers and brought them eternal hope.

May this book provoke us—like Harry Waggoner—to offer ourselves as living sacrifices so our Lord can touch those around us and lead them to a saving knowledge of Jesus Christ.

Hal Donaldson

1
"I'll Do Anything He Asks"

Pittsburgh, Pennsylvania, 1891. The Reverend John Waggoner, garbed in his black Western suit, ambled down the long dark hospital corridor that strangely resembled an unlit cavern. The nurses' iron faces were half-shadowed as they scurried from room to room. More than the bleak atmosphere, though, it was the unpleasant task before John that had transformed this place into a dungeon of sorts.

The heels of his boots clicked against the wood floor like a percussion instrument, the rhythmic beat bouncing off the pale walls. Before entering the hospital room of Miss Zella McCauley, John swallowed, inhaled deeply, and uttered a simple prayer: "God, I need Your help."

To John's surprise, his parishioner's cubicle defied the solemnness of everything outside her door. Her room was bright and festive, and the twenty-six-year-old patient smiled without compromise. Her thin face raised from the pillow as John stepped to her bedside.

"Good afternoon, Zella. How are you feeling?"

In a feeble but cheerful tone she said, "Pressing on, Pastor. I'm so glad I know Jesus."

John felt a single tear emerging in his eye. It seemed so unmerciful to dampen her spirits by conveying the news that she had six weeks to live, but the minister knew he could not shrug his responsibility. Better for her to hear it from him than for the spinal meningitis to send its own message.

"Zella, there's something you must know."

Before John could finish his thought, Zella interrupted. "Pastor, I know what you're going to say. The doctors decided to tell me this morning. They said there's nothing more they can do."

Without a word, John clasped her hand, his bottom lip shivering, trying to fend off a stream of tears.

Zella's eyes began to water as she said boldly, "Pastor, I'm ready to go. Someday soon I'll see Jesus face to face."

Suddenly, John's expression began teetering on a grin. "Yes, if it is your time, no doubt He'll be there to greet you."

John was about to whisper a prayer when a gentle knock interrupted his thoughts. Two elderly women wearing ankle-length dresses, black shawls, and bonnets entered the room. The smaller of the two asked, "Miss McCauley?"

"Yes, I'm Zella McCauley."

"We were given your name and asked to stop in and pray with you."

Zella said, "Yes, thank you. This is my pastor, Reverend Waggoner."

John nodded his head and smiled cordially.

The smaller woman opened her Bible and read, "Go ye into all the world, and preach the gospel to every creature . . . . These signs shall follow them that believe . . . . They shall lay hands on the sick, and they shall recover" (Mark 16:15-18).

With conviction in her voice and emphasis on the last syllable of each phrase, the other woman blurted, "We know that Jesus healed the sick in His daaaay, and we also believe He can do the same for us todaaay . . . if we will only belieeeeve."

John had heard of those who propagated the doctrine of divine healing, yet he remained skeptical of their teachings. After all, he had never seen indisputable evidence of anything resembling a miracle; he had just heard the usual rumors about cripples walking and the deaf hearing. But this was neither the time nor place to enter into a theological debate, so John joined the ladies by bowing his head in prayer for Zella.

The smaller woman said, "The Bible says we are to lay hands on the sick and pray, believing. Pastor, you believe in God's Word, don't you?"

"Why, yes; of course I believe it," he affirmed without raising his head.

Then, without pausing, she prayed, "Lord Jesus, You are the Great Physician . . . . Your power has never diminished . . . . You are the same yesterday, today, and forever. We ask in Your name to raise Your child out of this bed and make her whole. Thank You for hearing our prayer, and thank You for healing her. In the blessed name of Jesus, amen."

Opening his eyes, John didn't know what to expect. Surely Zella won't actually leap from her bed, he thought. Surely not.

When the two women exited, Zella had yet to display anything resembling a healing. She was still confined to her bed, and, to himself, John reaffirmed his doubts about the "faith movement."

The youthful Zella turned her head toward John, her shrinking eyes sluggish to follow. "Pastor Waggoner, do you really think God heard their prayer and that He might heal me?"

John didn't want to disappoint her, so he said, "I'm a preacher of the gospel, but this is all new to me, Zella. But I learned long ago that I shouldn't limit God."

Instantly, a measure of hope surfaced in the dimpled chin of the crimson-haired woman.

She said, "Maybe God still has something for me to do for Him. If He heals me, I'll do anything He asks me to. I mean it from the bottom of my heart, Pastor."

"I know you do, Zella."

John questioned whether this episode was, in retrospect, unfortunate, for he feared the two women had posed hopes in Zella that would soon be deflated. But who knows, John countered to himself, maybe there is something to praying for the sick after all.

Three days passed before John could get away from his day job as a butcher to revisit his dying parishioner. When he entered her room, her bed was empty. John rushed to the nurses' station, fearing the inevitable had occurred. "What happened to Miss McCauley?"

A plump woman in white, mounted behind a desk, reacted to his desperate question with an all-too-pleasant smile. "She's going home, sir. I think they're getting her ready now."

John turned away from the woman, then recoiled as she explained Zella's recovery. "It was the most amazing thing I'd ever seen—that young woman so near death, then being able to walk." Lifting her head from her desk to look John in the eye, she added, "Miss McCauley's telling everyone she was healed. Was she, Reverend?"

John hesitated before responding, "I'm not sure, but something miraculous must have happened. Prayer surely didn't hurt."

Deep in thought, sitting on a bench, John's five-foot-ten-inch frame bounced upright. Zella, flanked by two doctors, had just entered his view from the unlit hallway.

"Pastor, look at me. I'm healed!" she shouted with a measure of irreverence for the hospital wing's gloomy atmosphere. Surprisingly, the nurses did not attempt to thwart Zella's boisterous demonstration. And the two doctors grinned as if they had sanctioned her high-pitched outburst. John gazed with astonishment, unable to voice a single syllable.

"I'm going home!" she bellowed. "I'm well. I told God I would go to India to work with lepers if He wanted me to. So, now that I'm well, I'm going to India, Pastor."

John chuckled as his young convert bubbled with excitement. He examined her walk for the slightest limp or defect.

"Isn't God good, Pastor Waggoner?"

"Yes, He is. Yes, He sure is," the minister said, bobbing his head with bewilderment.

An hour later, John carried Zella's suitcase out the hospital corridor into the sunlight, pondering how he was going to explain this "miracle" on Sunday to a congregation that did not believe in miracles.

2
Called by God

Zella kept her promise to serve as a missionary to the lepers in India. And while home on furlough in 1901, she came to visit the Waggoners on their farm in Avalon, Pennsylvania—a small community west of Pittsburgh.

It was a warm but non-chastising afternoon when nine-year-old Harry Waggoner—John and Lulu's seventh of fourteen children—perched himself in a cherry tree across the path from the towering corn field. He was devouring the red fruit and sticking the pits in the pocket of his overalls when his father, mother, and Miss McCauley settled below his branch in lawn chairs. Harry remained silent, testing to see if he could eavesdrop on their conversation without being discovered.

Zella said with a sigh, "My heart still bleeds for India and the lepers there. Very little is being done for them, and I'm not sure how much longer I'll be able to carry on the work alone. I've been praying that God would lay it upon someone's heart . . . to commit his life to helping the lepers."

John and Lulu nodded their heads and pledged their prayers, not realizing God was speaking to their son nestled directly above them. Young Harry could not ignore the compelling words reverberating in his mind: "You will be that man; someday you will do My work among the lepers of India."

To himself, Harry vowed to obey the voice of God.

He listened intently as Zella told stories of the needy people she had left behind, the people she yearned to serve, the people Harry was now being called to help. For weeks after Zella and the Waggoners had chatted under his tree, Harry daydreamed of traveling to a foreign land. The mere thought of such an adventure made the bushy-haired youngster feel warm inside. Though he felt certain God had spoken to him, he neglected to tell anyone. He was afraid his explanation of an "inner voice" would only instigate an onslaught of badgering from his brothers and sisters.

In time, Harry dismissed the tree experience on his own, deeming it nothing more than youthful imagination. His dreams of doing missionary work were surrendered in order to help the family make ends meet. He left school after the eighth grade to work full-time on the family farm.

Shortly thereafter, at age fourteen, Harry became bedridden with pneumonia. John and Lulu feared they might lose another son. Years earlier Walter, their oldest, died of German measles, and Clyde, their second child, died of smallpox. John entered Harry's room one morning before the roosters crowed and knelt beside his son's bed.

"Heavenly Father," he prayed, "touch Harry's body. I know You have a work for him to do. Just as You healed Zella and others, please take care of my son."

Lulu stood in the doorway praying, her face shielded by her shivering hands.

Harry, lying on his back, also prayed silently after his father left the room. He decided to recommit his life to God that morning even if that meant serving Him in India among the lepers. "I will go," the teenager promised. "If that was really You, Lord, speaking to me in the tree, I will go to India."

Within a few days of whispering that prayer, Harry began to recover. He stood to his feet one autumn morning more determined than ever to obey the calling on his life.

3
Consecrated for Service

Although Harry was sincere in his vow to go to India, the lure of financial security was unyielding. Upon celebrating his eighteenth birthday, Harry was offered a lucrative opportunity as the apprentice for a local jeweler. For weeks a battle raged inside the young man, wanting to do God's will, yet not wanting to ignore a proposition that would ensure his financial future and help his family. Like a slave torn between freedom and loyalty to his master, Harry weighed his options.

Finally, he reported to his parents his decision: he would attend Nyack Bible Institute and enter the school's two-year missionary training program.

Nyack offered its share of challenges for young Harry, especially when students discovered his intention to be a missionary to India.

"So you're going to go where your bones will bleach on the hot sands," one student jeered. Others joined in the teasing.

"Mr. Missionary, you're going to ride the elephants?" another chortled.

Harry was not laughing. Their taunting merely fueled reservations already burning inside him.

"What have I committed myself to?" he asked softly. "Am I a fool to think a white man can make a difference in India?"

One night, after enduring another jeering session from his fellow students, he went to his room and started praying. "God, if You will lead me and open the way, I *will* go to Bombay, India. No one is going to scare me into breaking the promise I made to You."

With the devotion of a golden retriever chasing a falling bird, Harry set out to prepare himself for missionary work. There was one pleasant distraction, though. Her name was Helen Porter, a former kindergarten teacher he first met at a revival meeting in Ohio. But Harry initially had to smother his romantic intentions for Helen, who was "friendly" with another Nyack student. When Helen revealed to her boyfriend her calling to the mission field, however, that relationship proved to be short-lived. Seizing his chance, Harry began slipping letters from a "secret admirer" under her door.

One morning, while returning from breakfast, Helen noticed Harry delivering one of his love notes.

"Mr. Waggoner, may I help you?" she asked.

"Well, I was just . . . ." His face radiated with embarrassment. There were no creative explanations filling his mind, so he stammered, "I was putting a note under your door."

"About what?"

Harry paused, wondering if he should tell her or let her read the note for herself. Helen's owl-like eyes were hanging on his response. He thought, How foolish for me to think that a proper city girl like her would ever like a poor country boy like me.

Finally, he said, "I wanted to let you know how much I like you."

Harry braced himself for rejection, but the petite Helen was all smiles.

"I like you, too," she said awkwardly.

Harry squeezed her hand, grinned, then hastily retreated, thinking to himself that he had just fixed eyes on his future wife.

Harry and Helen were engaged to be married in June 1911. That summer Harry returned to his father's farm in Warren, Ohio, where John and Lulu pastored a small church. Helen, meanwhile, went to Youngstown, Ohio, where her father was an executive with the Baltimore and Ohio Railroad Company.

Harry's homecoming was bittersweet. He was unprepared for the verbal abuse that several parishioners directed toward his father. Zella McCauley's healing had triggered a transformation in John's ministry. He began praying for the sick and preaching messages that dealt with God's power and mercy. The angular minister often shed tears from his pulpit and spoke of God's compassion for the needy. But it was John and Lulu's stance on the baptism of the Holy Spirit that had created the most recent flap.

A few members from John's congregation and officials from his denomination were intent on keeping what they considered a "false doctrine" from poisoning the church.

Three days after Harry arrived home from school, a delegation of denominational leaders came to the Waggoner home unannounced. John met the group on the front porch, asking, "You have come to ask me to renounce my belief in the baptism of the Holy Spirit, haven't you?"

The spokesman shook his head affirmatively, saying, "John, come to your senses. This is not of God. If it was, don't you think the eldership would have accepted it?"

"Gentlemen, I refuse to deny what I know is the truth. If that's what you're demanding . . . then you can have my resignation."

A white-haired man with a sagging neck, said, "We don't want you to leave; simply restrict your teaching to the Word of God."

John's chin was steel. "You have my resignation."

"If you're telling us that you will not refrain from this practice," the man said with his head lowered, "then, yes, John, you will have to leave."

One by one, the visitors shook John's hand then piled into their vehicles like Old West circuit judges mounting their horses. John peered at them, fighting the temptation to become enraged, trying to fend off animosity and disappointment. He stared at the sky for a long while after his accusers' departure. He wanted to shout. He wanted to cry. But all he could do was stare without emotion.

Lulu stood by his side quietly caressing his arm. There was so much she wanted to share, but it was obvious that no words could relieve John's pain.

The Sunday following John's dismissal, a caravan of forty automobiles arrived at the Waggoner home to offer their support and hear more about the baptism of the Holy Spirit.

As car doors slammed outside the Waggoner house that Sabbath morning, John walked onto his front porch.

A robust farmer, donning a black hat and black tie, stepped forward. Removing his hat, he said, "Mornin', Reverend. We were wantin' to know what happened."

John overlooked the gathering like a pastor speaking from a pulpit. His left hand formed into a passive fist as he fought back the tears.

"Please, Pastor Waggoner, we want to know."

Gaining his composure, John said, "They removed me because of my belief in speaking in tongues."

The farmer came closer, distancing himself from the others. "But you're our pastor. And we believe like you. What right do they have to . . . ?"

"We'll just start our own church," another man urged. Others cheered the suggestion. Then, one after another, they handed their tithes and offerings to John, saying, "Here, it's God's will that you have this. You're our shepherd."

That summer John and a fledgling congregation, with Harry's assistance, held services in a simple A-frame building. Those few months before Harry returned to Nyack proved to be invaluable for the missionary student. He witnessed miracles and felt the presence of the Holy Spirit like never before.

Helen's parents, meanwhile, were not pleased with their daughter's involvement in the Pentecostal Movement. They were from an ancestral line of Episcopalians and viewed this "new" experience as emotionalism unfit for people of their educational background. They blamed Harry for Helen's "misguided" views and pleaded with their daughter to break off the engagement. They even begged her to reconsider her plans to serve in India.

But as the wedding day approached, the Porters threw up their hands and offered their blessing. On November 27, 1912, friends and family gathered at the Porters' home in Youngstown for the festive occasion.

During their first year as husband and wife, Harry and Helen assisted a pastor in Youngstown, still believing God would somehow make it possible for them to fulfill their calling to India. These were difficult months for the newlyweds, though, for the yearning to minister abroad intensified with each passing day.

"Sometimes I wonder why we're here when we're needed in India," Harry confessed.

Helen nodded her head. "I know, but we must be patient. When God wants us there, He'll provide a way."

Harry glanced at his spouse as if to say, "I know; but I hope it's soon."

In November 1913, Harry and Helen, who was five months pregnant at the time, reserved passage on the S. S. Berlin destined for Bombay, India. There they would enroll in a language school to learn Hindi. The young missionaries were not certain where they would serve, or in what capacity, yet they made plans to sail to the despairing land, believing God would lead them to their niche of ministry.

They saved money and worked extra jobs to pay their passage to India, but as the day of their departure approached they were fifty dollars shy of what was needed to pay the fare. Harry had refused to borrow funds from his family, and Helen was certain hers would not help. Harry and his bride said, "If God wants us to go, He's going to provide."

As the young couple lugged their bags up the docks, they were still lacking the needed funds. The first boarding call had already been announced. Still, Harry and Helen waited. The second boarding call came, and the young couple peered at one another afraid to think their trip would have to be postponed.

Without warning, a fellow student nudged Harry. The classmate said, "God wanted me to give you this." He placed three bills totaling fifty dollars into Harry's hand.

Helen burst into tears.

Harry's eyelids had already accumulated moisture when he said, "I don't know when I can repay you."

The young man said, "Don't worry, God will. This is a gift."

Helen smeared her tears across her cheeks and began gleaming like an angel. "God bless you!" she said.

As the ship disembarked, Harry could not help but feel a sliver of regret for having to leave his family. Staring at the billows, he reflected on the farewell service held at his father's church several days ago. After Harry had preached that night, his father stepped to the pulpit and embraced him. John then prayed, "God, thank You for a son who has

been obedient to Your voice. Protect him . . . And . . . ."
John could no longer restrain his emotions; the tears vying
for his cheeks erupted.

The longer Harry peered at the water, the more he
wondered if he would ever see his parents again. "Was the
emotional farewell our final meeting?" he asked. That
thought sent a distressing shiver down the spine of his
six-foot-two-inch frame.

Before leaving, Harry and Helen learned there were no
openings for leper work; that uncertainty alone threatened
to supersede the joy of finally setting out for India.

Harry's eyes were fixed on the water as he pondered the
future and the family he was leaving behind. Helen,
sensing his melancholy mood, leaned on his shoulder along
the railing. "Harry, don't worry. God has called us and
that's all that matters."

"I know. I'm just going to miss Ohio and all our family
and friends."

Helen slid her hand into his and said, "Me too. But
someday we'll see them again."

Harry thought to himself, I only hope she is right.

4
"Together We Will Make a Difference!"

Copper-skinned women in sarees and men wearing thin cotton skirts surrounded the gangplank as the ocean liner's passengers disembarked in Bombay. Dark children with the widest smiles imaginable reached to carry the Waggoners' suitcases. Bombay—a far cry from Warren, Ohio—was a stirring city with rickshaws, bicycles, and pedestrians jostling for their share of dirt roads.

The British influence was obvious in the architecture, food, entertainment, and clothing. But many customs and traits—the generous smiles, inflection of their voices, and religious rituals—were unmistakably Indian.

Shortly after his arrival, Harry was invited to accompany a missionary to a religious fair. Thousands were worshiping at a large Mohammedan tomb, chanting and bowing at prescribed intervals.

"Who are those people?" Harry pointed. "The ones with the layers of clothing."

"The lepers," his missionary friend said. "They aren't permitted inside, so they congregate outside to worship their god."

For the first time Harry's eyes fell on the people he had come to serve. He carefully studied their garments and slithering movements, grappling with feelings of anticipation and sorrow. Their bodies were mummied in cloth. Only their glinting eyes could be seen under their brown hoods and scarfs.

"Where are you going?" the missionary asked as Harry skirted away.

"I'm going to go talk to the lepers."

"What! Harry, wait a minute. Don't you know that leprosy is infectious?"

"I know. I'm just going to talk to them."

The missionary wagged his head incredulously.

With that, the two men maneuvered closer to the rows of lepers. They decided to wait until the worshipers completed their rituals before entering the kneeling pack. As the two missionaries wiped perspiration from their brows, they saw servants prepare to wash the tomb. Instantly, like school children fleeing their desks for the playground, the lepers rose to leave.

"Where are they going?" Harry asked, puzzled by the sudden stampede.

"They're going to a pool where the water used to wash the tomb will drain. Since the water has touched the tomb, they believe that it is holy and will heal them of their disease."

The sight of these monk-like robes hobbling to the murky puddle brought tears to Harry's eyes. He had dreamed of their plight—the open and corrupt ulcers, the stumps for hands and feet, the hoarse voices, and the indescribable disfigured features—but this flight toward ordinary water had turned the spigot of Harry's emotions. This entire scene strongly reminded him of the "leper's squint" he had researched—a small aperture through which those stricken with the terrible disease could view the services in England's Fourth Century St. Martin's Cathedral.

In India, where the caste system determines whether one will be a slave or a king, the leper is stripped of all stature.

"Jesus is their only hope," Harry whispered under a waterfall of tears. "Now I know why Jesus had such pity on the lepers when they came to Him for cleansing, and why He was moved with such compassion."

"That's why we're here," the other missionary reflected. "There's one-quarter of a million lepers in India. They wander in and out of villages seeking someone, anyone, who will spare a few grains of rice and show them compassion. They hold out their fingerless hands in hopes that someone will ease their hunger pangs. It breaks your heart, doesn't it?"

Harry stood speechless.

The following day the aspiring missionary found himself weary from a sleepless evening of tossing in bed. Visions of vagabond lepers had danced in his mind until morning. He could not escape the mental images inscribed on his memory: a leprous old man whose food had been carried off by a pye dog, and a woman who was wallowing in filth had no one to wash her clothes or give her medicine. They had, undoubtedly, been abandoned by their families, left to beg until they fell victim to their disease. Another man, who was crawling around on all fours, brushed away the pesky flies that tormented his exposed flesh.

It staggered Harry to realize that 400 million lived in India without knowing Jesus Christ. But when he heard 30,000 were dying each day, many of whom were lepers, a sense of urgency gripped him. Now he understood why so many lepers attempted to end their misery by throwing themselves into the river.

More distressing scenes were about to be engraved in Harry's mind. Some days later, he and Helen set out for Muttra, a holy city of 60,000 inhabitants. Their carriage came to a halt on the outskirts of the city as they encountered a legion of Hindu lepers who had descended on Muttra seeking deliverance from their sins and freedom from their disease. As the Waggoners observed the lepers surrounding the burning ghats—a bonfire where dead bodies are consumed—they yearned ever more deeply for the day they could befriend these outcasts and offer them hope as full-time missionaries.

The couple eventually moved to Dhond, a small town in the Poona District, to assist in an orphanage until a more permanent appointment in a leper colony became available. Here Harry worked as a colporteur, selling Bibles to pay for their language schooling and living expenses. Harry was like a caravan merchant the way he proudly held the reins to the horse-drawn wagon that carried his evangelism tent and Bibles. Until God led them elsewhere, the young couple traveled from village to village holding evangelism services under the "big top." Although the Waggoners were gradually learning the language, an interpreter and several layworkers graciously accompanied them to their meetings.

One evening on the trail, while asleep in his tent, Harry was awakened by something crawling on his feet. The tickling sensation propelled him outside in seconds. Hundreds of white ants had crawled onto his body. Peeling off his clothes, Harry raced into the moonlight. When he returned from his scamper, wearing only his underwear, he was met by Helen and some of the natives. They did all they could to contain their giggles.

"Look at you. What in the world?" Helen declared.

Harry darted back inside the tent to be certain the ants hadn't nibbled on his Bibles. Throwing a blanket around his body, he exclaimed, "I was being eaten alive by ants!"

The natives must have understood his explanation, for, without even a simple interpretation, they proceeded to laugh themselves to sleep.

March hit like a forest fire, the sun's rays beating down unabatedly. This particular year, so the natives said, was hotter than most. It was especially miserable for Helen who was eight and one-half months pregnant. March was the beginning of the hot season, though for Westerners the entire year seemed blistering. During the months when the sun normally dominates one's thoughts, temperatures reached 115 degrees in the shade. By the time morning came, Harry and Helen found themselves sleeping in a puddle of perspiration, their hair moistened as if they had run through a light drizzle.

Wet washcloths draped Helen's forehead and her clothes were sticking to her skin when she yelled, "Harry!"

Harry casually lumbered to her bedside.

"What can I get you?" he asked sympathetically.

"A doctor," Helen said.

Harry's eyes swelled.

"Stay here," he stuttered. "Stay here. I'll be right back."

With the desperation of a hunted animal, Harry dashed off to collect their local physician. Several hours later, Helen gave birth to Willard, an eight-pounder who was born wearing a smile. He was their first child, their little prince, their gift from God.

While the Waggoners were resting in the Himalaya Mountains some months later, where it was cool and refreshing, Willard was nearly snatched from them. The growing child was playing in the middle of the floor of their bungalow when Helen motioned for the little one to crawl to her. As Willard scooted in the direction of his mother, a section of the ceiling began to cave in. A large concrete beam landed where the baby had been playing.

Thinking the whole apartment was collapsing, Helen championed her bundle outside. Harry intercepted them on the porch.

"What happened?" he asked with a startled tone.

"The ceiling collapsed, but thank God Willard is safe!" she said, squeezing the child even tighter.

Harry's eyes flicked from Helen to the baby, then cautiously examined the ceiling.

Later that evening, while bouncing Willard on his lap, Harry's thoughts drifted from the horrifying incident to their months of waiting for an appointment to a leper colony. They had enjoyed serving at the orphanage and distributing Bibles, but it was not their ultimate calling. Recent days had been distressing and doubt-filled, and they wondered if they had mistaken God's instructions. Harry looked at his tattered shoes, which had traveled many dirt roads, then said to his infant son, "Maybe we didn't hear from the Lord after all."

Helen, normally a quiet girl with deep convictions, entered the room in time to hear her husband's groaning. She said, "Reverend Waggoner, we heard from God and He knows what He's doing!"

Her husband's reaction was stately. "Woman, I know that. Aren't I allowed to ever release my frustrations?"

"Of course you are," Helen smiled. "I was just offering a simple reminder."

Harry smirked. "Reminder accepted."

A week after that exchange, a messenger boy came to the door with a telegram from Baitalpur in the Central Provinces. It was a formal offer for Harry to become superintendent of a leper asylum.

Harry embraced his wife, the telegram crumpling against her back.

"God has answered our prayers!" Harry proclaimed loudly into her unguarded ear.

"I knew He would," she said, stopping short of saying, "I told you so."

Even Willard let out a timely, gleeful yelp.

The lovers looked at one another then pressed their cheeks together as if to say, "The months of questioning are over. Together we will make a difference!"

5
Rough Beginnings

Wild animals galloped and villagers waved as the train sped toward Baitalpur. On board was one of the youngest couples ever to be appointed superintendents of an asylum this size: in excess of 600 lepers. Because of the growing tensions in 1913, on the threshold of World War I, the German missionaries who had established the facility were ordered home. Since then, the asylum had gone through several directors. The most recent director had been forced to leave because of illness. Desperately in need of a replacement, the board of directors offered the assignment to twenty-three-year-old Harry.

As Harry and Helen walked into the chapel of their asylum, they were momentarily stunned by the sight of these pitiful specimens of humanity. Here the lepers did little to conceal their affliction; their deteriorating faces and eroding limbs were freely exposed. Their voices had a hollow, hoarse quality, yet they were singing hymns in Hindi with such conviction.

The two missionaries stood at the rear of the sanctuary. Harry saw this room of dying flesh as the fruition of his cherry tree experience. Helen merely closed her eyes. For her, too, this was the culmination of a lifelong dream.

But their fairy tale would have to be postponed. Shortly after their arrival, an outbreak of cholera and typhoid forced Harry and Helen to relocate until the epidemic had run its course and their second child was born. They reluctantly left behind their vision of ministry and their new flock.

Lois was born December 17, 1915. The four-pound child was born with a caul, which was of great interest to the superstitious natives. To them it meant the child had been granted a special blessing by the gods. Upon returning to the asylum, Harry and Helen found the lepers and native workers celebrating, laughing, eating, and thanking their Hindu gods for blessing the Waggoners with such an unusual child.

The celebration was short-lived, however, for the child grew weaker with each passing day. She weighed only thirteen pounds after eight months.

Lois lived only nine and one-half months before succumbing to an unknown disorder. Harry managed to rise above the ordeal as well as could be expected, but Helen was not herself for several months. She could not help but believe the child had contracted an avoidable illness, and thus the young mother wrestled with the illegitimate shame many parents experience when faced with this type of tragedy.

Harry often awakened during the night and found Helen crying into her blanket. He tried to comfort her, to unlock a biblical secret that would soothe her pain. Seldom did it do any good.

"God will give us another child, dear. Our little girl is in heaven with the Lord."

Inevitably, Helen's eyes gushed with tears until she exhausted herself to sleep.

That scene repeated itself for weeks.

Without Lois, Helen began to devote a majority of her time to Willard. One afternoon, the prized son nearly brought further grief to his mourning mother. Playing in the middle of the floor with wooden toys carved by the natives, Willard was full of life and fun. Helen left the room momentarily to pour him a cup of buffalo milk. She returned to find her only son pointing toward the hideous figure of a cobra. The serpent's neck was arched as it slithered within the child's reach. Willard appeared unruffled, thinking it was just another toy. Helen inched her way out the door and summoned the aid of an Indian who played a homemade flute. As the notes echoed from the man's instrument, the cobra maneuvered toward the flutist and out the door, where it was immediately killed.

Some weeks after he had settled into his new role as director of the Baitalpur asylum, Harry went to visit a prominent Indian businessman in the region.

"Why don't the relatives of these lepers try to do something for them? Why do they desert them like they do?" the missionary asked.

The man, dressed in a sleek Western suit, lowered his tea cup. "Because, sir, lepers have committed the unpardonable sin. The gods have chosen to punish them in this way. If we try to help them, we are interfering with the work of the gods."

Harry suddenly realized why God had sent *him*, a white man, to India. Many Indians were taught to disown the leper, but a Caucasian, not bound by their taboos, could make a difference. And so it was that Harry and Helen set out to expose lepers to the love of Jesus Christ.

One morning, Helen woke with her back feeling as raw as a slimy trout. At first she feared she had contracted a mysterious illness, but she was relieved to discover it was what the natives called "prickly heat," a symptom that passes like the common cold. While Helen was recovering, Harry and one of the native workers went shopping for another plow horse for the asylum's farmland. Just before sundown, Harry bounced up the steps to their apartment and asked Helen to peer out her bedroom window at the animal he had purchased.

She drew back the makeshift curtain and angled her head. "It's beautiful, dear. How much did it cost?"

"Don't worry; well within what we could afford."

The black creature with a thick mane looked strong and healthy, but Helen knew very little about such matters. Harry was the farmhand.

"I've already given it a name," Harry announced.

"Oh, you have?"

"Yes; how does 'Joshua' sound?"

"A Bible name for a horse?"

"Why not?" Harry chuckled.

Helen's head fell back onto the mattress, amused by her husband's childlike love for animals.

"You'd better get him under a roof," Helen said, referring to the forthcoming rains.

The next morning brought no foreboding sign that the weather pattern was about to change, but the natives assured their pastors there would be flooding in the streets within hours.

Pointing to the street, one of the helpers said, "It will be like a river here."

"When?" Harry asked.

"Soon," the man warned, lifting his cotton dhoti or loin cloth well above his ankles as if wading through water.

Harry laughed, skeptical of his friend's prediction.

Their conversation was interrupted when a young boy came running, shouting, "Josh-wa gone. Josh-wa gone."

"Where? Gone where?" Harry asked, bending to read the boy's eyes.

"Josh-wa gone."

"Yes, but where?"

"Josh-wa gone."

Harry realized the boy could not understand English. Addressing the lad in broken Hindustani, Harry discovered that Joshua had run away. A disheartened Harry patted the youngster's shiny head, realizing he would probably never see the beloved horse again. In cities like this, unclaimed horses were often snatched by black marketeers.

The missionary soon discovered the severity of the rains. The downpour formed a mote two feet deep in front of the asylum, and, as predicted, Harry was traipsing through the water, pulling up his trousers.

While the young couple was learning to cope with the monsoon, one of the staff members received notification that her fiance, a Norwegian, had died of cholera in his home country. The young girl had already been fitted for her wedding dress, and arrangements had been made for Harry to conduct the ceremony. The girl's wailing continued from dusk to dawn, rousing the lepers from their mats. Rushing to the grieving girl's room, Helen often cradled her in her arms, brushed back her hair, and offered soothing proverbs.

Her mourning carried on for a week before she knocked on the Waggoners' door.

"Yes, Sally, are you doing better today?" Helen asked.

"A little; is Pastor Waggoner here?"

"Right here," he announced from his chair.

The young girl stuttered as she began to speak. "I . . . I . . . I want to ask you something."

In a gentle voice, Harry nodded, "Surely."

"I would like your permission to return to America."

Her eyes glanced at Harry, then Helen, for a reaction.

"Sister, if you feel God is leading you . . . ."

"I'm just not sure I can survive here without . . . ."

Emotions burst from her before she could explain, but Harry and Helen understood her reasons.

Helen wrapped her arms around Sally, and with two pats said, "It's okay, dear. Let it out."

Harry said, "Sister, if you believe God wants you to leave, then certainly you may leave. But be sure it is God calling you home."

"Thank you," she said, bowing her head, wiping her tears, and retreating out the front door.

A few days later, Sally climbed onto a buggy to be taken to the train station. Harry and Helen waved farewell with pleasant faces, though knowing they were going to be left shorthanded.

As Helen reflected on Sally's fiance—a handsome man who visited the asylum eight weeks before his death—the thought of losing *her* man invaded her introspective moment. "God, what would I do without Harry?" she asked. "Protect him, dear Father." She stared at her spouse with loving respect and repeated, "Please protect him."

The monsoon came and went, and the snakes fled their holes. Sixty snakes of all shapes and colors, including three cobras, were killed at the asylum that year, the largest measuring nearly seven feet.

Helen was sweeping out their sleeping quarters when she spotted something slithering along the floor next to their bed. The trunk of the reptile was the size of a man's forearm. She backed out of the room without incident and ran to the chapel where Harry was praying.

She was out of breath when she arrived, but the wild expression in her eyes let Harry know something terrible had frightened her.

"What is it?" he asked.

"A snake, in our bedroom, large," Helen gasped.

Harry grabbed a shotgun and led a band of natives across the courtyard to confront the intruder. The workers managed to lure the snake out of the apartment by waving a stick, and Harry fired two well-placed shots.

The natives were clapping their hands and patting Harry's back when Helen asked, "Is it dead?"

Harry smiled proudly as his rooting section surrounded him. "They don't call me 'the hunter' for nothing, you know."

"Well, could there be more snakes?" she asked.

A stout man wearing a turban and slurping down a piece of a mango answered, "There's no worry here; Pastor Waggoner have gun."

"Like he says, dear," Harry added confidently, "I'll keep my anointed shotgun by my side at all times."

6
Shattered Dreams

Over the next five years, the Waggoner family grew. Helen gave birth to Donald in 1917, followed by two daughters: Beatrice in 1919, and Almeta in 1920.

Their stay in Baitalpur had been an invaluable period of becoming acquainted with the customs and beliefs of the Indian people. But one conviction simmered in Harry's thoughts day after day: he believed lepers should have a home, something more than an impersonal dormitory-asylum like that near Baitalpur. Harry longed to establish a facility that gave the leper a shred of self-respect. He wanted to create a mission where each leper could have a separate home with a personal garden. And he dreamed of having an orphanage in the compound so the "clean" children of leprous parents could be nearby.

One morning Harry feared his dreams were in jeopardy when he noticed a rash on his arm. He hid the news from Helen until he could have a physician examine the spot. He could not help but wonder if his close contact with lepers had rendered him one of them.

Whenever a sore appeared on a native's skin, Harry checked to see if it was leprous by sticking it with a pin. If the individual felt pain, then it wasn't leprosy because the disease typically kills the nerve endings in the skin. Even though he felt the pin pierce his skin when he administered the crude test on himself, Harry feared the rash was the beginning stages of the dreaded disease. He could not rest until he had a professional opinion.

After the local doctor examined Harry's skin, the balding man clapped his hands and convulsed with laughter.

"No, Reverend Waggoner, it's not leprosy. It's something quite common around here. You have what they call 'dhoGi's itch.'"

Relieved by the doctor's diagnosis, Harry asked, "What causes it?"

"It's from the soap used to wash your clothes. It's quite common, believe me, especially among the launderers or 'dhoGis.' I must see several cases a month and usually much worse than yours."

By 1921, the Waggoners were far too familiar with death. As many as 150 lepers died during a year, many stricken with cholera. Nothing, however, tested their strength and faith like the flu epidemic that was sweeping the world.

Harry conducted countless funerals, sometimes several in one day, all the while knowing his own strength was diminishing. Sharp pains pierced his chest, stealing whatever stamina he had. His stately frame had shriveled to 135 pounds. He feared his condition was serious and deserving of sophisticated care, yet he did not want to leave the people who depended on him for help. He knew his duty was not done. The lepers needed care. They needed Jesus. So he said nothing to anyone.

Helen begged her husband to rest, to reduce his workload. He ignored her pleas, occasionally traipsing to bed just before dawn, his haggard body dropping to his mattress.

At the gravesite of one leper, Harry's speech became slow. He felt his sense of balance failing and stuck out his arms like a child trying to tip-toe across a wooden beam. Suddenly, he collapsed in the middle of his prayer.

Helen—gripped by terror—let out a shrill. The native workers loaded his feeble body onto an oxcart and took him to a British doctor.

Helen prayed all the way to the doctor's office, frequently glancing over her shoulder to be certain Harry was breathing. She slumped to her knees outside the examination room. "God, preserve him. We have so much yet to do here. Heal him of whatever this is. Please, Father."

An hour after Harry was admitted, Helen was still praying. "Mrs. Waggoner," the doctor interrupted, tapping her on the shoulder. She jolted to her feet.

The doctor's face registered the worst.

Helen asked, "How is he?"

"Well, his heart is beating irregularly, but that might improve if he's given a lengthy rest."

"Is there anything we can do?" asked Helen, her ears primed for every word.

"I'll be frank. If you don't get him out of India soon, you're going to bury him here."

Helen's faith pulsated as she pondered how disappointed her husband would be when he heard the diagnosis. Moreover, she thought of the fate of the lepers who depended on them for survival. And what about those who had given their lives to Christ? she asked herself. Would they continue in the faith after she and her husband were gone? Finally, she resolved that it was in God's hands and they had no choice but to return to the States to recuperate.

Before leaving for Bombay for the voyage to America, Harry wanted to visit the chapel one last time. As he entered through the side door, he heard the lepers singing a song he had taught them. Within moments the lepers began to weep, and the music stopped. Harry tried to speak from the podium, but he was too weak and too shaken to explain his feelings. With tears coursing down his cheeks, he waved farewell and boarded an oxcart laden with his wife, children, and their few cherished belongings.

"Sahib," a native worker asked, "will you come back?"

"Only God knows for sure, but we hope so!"

With each mile on the road to Bombay, Harry posed the native's question to himself: "Will we ever come back?" At a moment of inner confrontation, he answered to himself: "It's unlikely we'll ever see Baitalpur again."

Once on board the freighter, Harry stationed himself on the deck facing the beloved land he was leaving behind. He stood there gazing, wondering if he would ever return, wondering if he was seeing his dream of ministry to the lepers fade as quickly as the shoreline in the distance.

7
Touched by God

John and Lulu Waggoner were struck with astonishment as they witnessed their fatigued son and his family climbing the porch to their house. Harry was pale, thin, and had aged beyond their expectations. They also marveled at their grandchildren. Grandma Waggoner unveiled a special treat for the occasion: a chocolate cake.

"You must be Beatrice?" Lulu asked, rubbing the back of the child's head.

Little Beatrice angled her head to show she didn't understand.

"Does a cat have your tongue?" Lulu laughed.

"Mother," Harry said, "she speaks Hindi. She doesn't know English too well yet!"

Lulu's expression seemed to ask, "What's Hindi?"

While his children licked their fingers and drank milk, Harry described the symptoms that had made it necessary for him to return home: the sleepless nights, the headaches, the heart pains. John was still pastoring the Pentecostal church in Warren and enjoying a new building that they had constructed on West Market Street. John was tiring, however, and he hoped Harry would stay and be his replacement once his son regained his health.

Harry, on the other hand, had his own aspirations. Someday, he hoped he would return to build a leper home. He had visions of resuming the work in Baitalpur, but he knew the Evangelical Church did not permit their missionaries to return to the same area once they left on furlough. The denomination believed the interim missionary process was counterproductive because it put everything on hold until the senior missionary returned from furlough. Nevertheless, Harry hoped his case would be the exception.

Some weeks passed, and Harry was beginning to show signs of improvement. Helen, on the other hand, was suffering with an ongoing case of nausea, so John took her to the doctor.

"Congratulations, Mrs. Waggoner," said the physician. "You're pregnant."

"Are you sure?" she asked, her jaw dropped.

"Quite sure."

"But . . . you're sure?"

"Yes, in about seven months you'll have another one crawling around."

John teased his son that afternoon, saying, "You're not as sick as you thought."

Helen turned her head with embarrassment. Harry smiled, thinking, I only wish that was true.

Too weak to stand for any length of time, Harry was still unable to accept speaking engagements. Furthermore, he was not well enough to visit his father-in-law in Youngstown, so Helen and the kids went alone for a weekend excursion.

Mr. Porter still had not accepted his daughter's faith, nor had he given his approval of her Pentecostal missionary work. Helen had written him twice a month for nearly seven years without receiving one response. She felt as though she had been disinherited and, as a result, feared how her father would respond to her and the children coming for a visit. Helen's mother died of a liver disorder several years earlier at age sixty-one. It grieved Helen that her mother would not be there to greet her grandchildren, nor would she be on hand to ensure that her husband behaved kindly in front of them.

The Waggoner clan flocked to their grandfather's door before Helen had a chance to properly introduce them. The old man was virtually mobbed when he admitted he was indeed their grandfather.

Dressed in a tailored suit, he calmly said, "Helen."

"Father," she responded dryly.

"It's good to see you."

"It's good to see you, Father."

The kids were tugging on his leg and arm, and he was about to fall when he gently shook them from their grasps.

Helen intervened. "Listen, children, that's enough. Now come inside and we'll get acquainted in a proper way."

The children filed inside like a platoon. Mr. Porter tendered no smile or pleasantries, but Helen knew she had finally made progress when her father welcomed them into his home. It was obvious the children had captured his affection.

Rising to her feet to say goodbye, Helen's hazel eyes met those of her father. Tears spilled from her eyes onto his shoulder as they embraced. She said, "I missed you."

"I missed you, too," he said. "I'm sorry we .... You've done well. These children are beautiful."

"They're a gift from God," she noted.

"That they are, and so are you."

When Helen returned to Warren, she bubbled with the news of her reconciliation with her father. While she rambled on, Harry appeared preoccupied. He also had something he was anxious to report. God had revealed to him in a dream the layout of a leper home that one day he and Helen were going to build in India.

Helen wanted to believe the dream was a message from God, but when she perused Harry's face—the sunken, sickly eyes—she feared it was nothing more than his imagination. Regardless of her feelings, she smiled at his announcement.

Four months passed, and Harry's return to health seemed to be at an impasse. His condition had improved, but he was still suffering with shortness of breath and chest pain. He was wrestling with discouragement for other reasons as well. The Evangelical Church rejected his bid to return to Baitalpur, so rather than go to another facility, the missionary submitted his resignation to the denomination.

The days that followed were distressing as Harry contemplated his "bleak" future.

Just when he seemed the lowest, a letter arrived from missionary Margaret Flint, urging him to attend a missions convention in Cleveland, Ohio. Harry perked with enthusiasm at the thought of seeing old friends and reveling in missionary stories, but his condition was prohibitive. He knew that tackling such a journey could jeopardize his recovery.

"Helen!" he called from his room. "Helen!"

"Yes, what do you need?" she answered.

"It's hard to explain. I just feel like I'm supposed to go to that missions convention. I think God wants me there."

"Do you think you're up to traveling alone? I don't think I should ride the train with me carrying our baby," she said, patting her stomach.

"I'm not sure, but I have to try."

"If God wants you there, you'll have the strength," she assured him.

A week before the convention, Harry complained of more chest pain and dismissed such a tiresome journey. But, somehow, on the day of the opening session, Harry found himself on a train en route to Cleveland.

Upon arriving at the large church that hosted the convention, Harry regretted that his late start caused him to miss the beginning of the evening service. Worship and music reverberated into the streets surrounding the building. Bundled in his warmest coat, Harry squeezed inside the overflow area—the building's basement. Because of the large turnout, they had been forced to hold a concurrent service downstairs. Believers knelt on the concrete floor; others sang with their hands raised. In front of a temporary pulpit, persons waited in line to receive prayer. Suddenly, Harry spotted Margaret in the middle of the healing line. He meandered toward her, then stopped. Harry knew Margaret suffered with a grapefruit-sized goiter that protruded from her neck. Harry watched as they laid hands on her, and, miraculously, he saw that growth shrink.

Falling to his knees in the aisle, Harry began praying. "God, if You can heal Margaret, You can do the same for my weakened body. Heal my heart of this disorder so I can return to India as Your servant."

Instantly, he felt a warmth in his chest, as if Someone reached down and gently massaged his heart. He stood to his feet and inhaled deeply without pain for the first time in many months. Like a whimpering child reaching for the soothing touch of a parent, Harry raised his hands to his Healer.

The following afternoon, he relayed his healing to A. G. Ward, a prominent pastor of an Assemblies of God church in Canada. At that time Harry also shared his vision for a leper home in India. Pastor Ward, a professional-looking man with a courteous smile, studied Harry's eyes as though grading his new friend's sincerity.

"Where would you build this leper home?" Reverend Ward asked.

"That I don't know."

"How are you going to finance such an undertaking?"

"God hasn't told me that yet. But He has spoken to my heart and given me a vision. I know He'll provide."

"Well, Reverend Waggoner, I appreciate your heart. You will be hearing from me soon." The elder preacher shook the missionary's hand and departed. Harry was filled with optimism that someone—perhaps Brother Ward—would lend financial support to a leper home.

When Harry's train screeched to a halt in Warren, he deboarded into Helen's waiting arms as words of thanksgiving spewed from his mouth. "God healed me! I felt God heal me, and I am breathing and eating and sleeping without pain."

Helen's mind reeled as she tried to absorb her husband's rapid succession of words.

"And A. G. Ward, an Assemblies of God minister, is interested in our plan for a leper home. He said he would contact us. God has healed me! Isn't it wonderful?"

Shaking her head, a wide-eyed Helen latched onto his arm with unusual authority. Inside she hoped he had truly been healed, for it would signal a new beginning for Harry and an end to her tribulation as well. Yet, she reserved her exuberance for fear of having to deal with another disappointment. To herself, she asked, "God, have You really touched Harry? Is this the work of Your hand? Are You preparing to send us back to the people of India?"

She watched Harry carefully the following days for any sign of pain. This was not Helen's way of exhibiting doubt as much as it was her way of discerning the will of God. She wanted to be certain Harry had fully recuperated before setting her sights on a return voyage to India.

8
Waiting for a Sign

Since Harry's conversation with A. G. Ward, months had passed. He feared that avenue of support had proven to be no more than a dead end. Harry and Helen, nevertheless, had remained confident God wanted them to return to India.

Yet, as nightfall came one October day, they began to tangle with confusion. In a rare moment they even wondered if they had been forgotten by God.

Even though they were living behind John and Lulu in a chicken coop that was converted into a small frame house, they spent much of their time alone. This afforded them time to doubt, time to trust.

"Helen," Harry asked while they were washing the supper dishes, "do you ever wonder if we were mistaken as to God's plan for our lives?"

"Some . . . times I do," she said.

Her frank response caught Harry by surprise. He could see his question had moved her to tears. He instantly wished he had not broached the subject.

She said, "I just want to go back so much. The lepers need us."

Harry tossed his dish towel and let Helen fall against his chest. Running his fingers through her hair, he said, "God knows, Honey. He knows what He is doing."

She cried long after Harry had wiped tears from her cheeks. Patiently, Harry held her in his arms. "Dear God," he prayed, "please show us that You are still with us. We need to know we haven't misinterpreted Your will."

"Yes, dear Jesus," Helen said.

"We need to know You are with us."

"Help us," she added softly. "We love You. We want to serve You. Surely You healed Harry for a reason. Please show us what You would have us do, where You want us to go."

With Harry's health fully restored, he was able to return to the work force. The family moved to Youngstown where Harry found temporary employment. The well-groomed home they rented was on the edge of the woods, so the children made a pastime of picking blackberries and reveling in their new playground filled with trees and wildlife.

After Doris was born, the children made a habit of gathering around their new sister's cradle. Whenever Donald or one of the others poked their finger at the baby's nose, Willard slapped away their pesky hands.

"Don't you know you could make the baby's face grow funny and give her germs by doing that?"

Harry was looking over their shoulders, feeling as though he was standing on top of the world. He was feeling like himself again, he had another child, his wife was healthy, and he had new hopes of returning to help the people he loved.

The sign, the direction, the couple had prayed for came sometime later in a letter from A. G. Ward: "Rev. and Mrs. Waggoner, I feel God has a purpose for you here in

Toronto. Will you come as my guests? There is much I wish to share with you about returning to India."

Ten days later, the family boarded a train for Toronto.

A. G. Ward was a motivator, an entrepreneur of God's work. And when he proposed ideas, one had the impression they eventually would become a reality. By the time the Waggoners reached Toronto, one of Pastor Ward's ideas—to form an organization to help the lepers—had already come to fruition. A board of directors had been established and plans were underway. "This board," Pastor Ward told Harry, "will help oversee and raise support for the leper home you have been called by God to build."

As A. G. Ward shared his plan, tears trickled down the Waggoners' faces.

"How can we thank you?" Harry said.

"Build that home, that's how!" A. G. Ward said with the charisma of an admiral.

"With God's help we will!"

"I know you will. Now I have several churches lined up for you to speak at before you return to India. Are you physically up to it?"

"I'm not much of a fundraiser, Brother Ward."

"You don't have to be. Just tell the people exactly what you shared with me. Tell them what God has laid upon your heart."

Harry glanced at his wife, then looked back at the Reverend Ward. "If it means helping the lepers, I'll do my best."

Paying their passage to India and purchasing the land for the leper home would require about $8,000. Although he would need the help of churches to reach their financial goal, Harry had strong reservations about asking congregations for money. "It just isn't my way," he insisted to Helen on several occasions. "I don't feel comfortable begging for money."

"You don't have to beg. Just tell them what we believe God is asking us to do," she said with quiet confidence. "Honey, you'll do fine."

"It's just not my way."

"You'll do fine," she repeated.

Harry was still reeling with doubt when he arrived at a church in Canada. He was an unusually shy man, especially for a preacher. Without fanfare the youthful-looking minister slipped in the back of the sanctuary, and there he waited patiently to meet the pastor. Meanwhile, as the starting time for the service approached, several deacons huddled together with anxious expressions on their faces, intermittently glancing at their watches. They were awaiting the guest speaker—surely a veteran missionary with perhaps a graying beard and wrinkles butterflying from his eyes. Harry remained silent and unassuming, hoping one of the deacons manning the back door would eventually offer a handshake. Finally, moments before the service, Harry introduced himself to the sentries.

"So you're Reverend Waggoner?" a tall thin man asked, rubbing one eye to hide his embarrassment.

"Yes," Harry said graciously.

"You are much younger than I expected."

Harry smiled, then followed his escort to the platform.

When Harry stepped to the pulpit, a stanza of whispers swished across the congregation as parishioners commented to their neighbors about his youthful appearance.

Harry smiled, then began conveying how he had been called to India. He shared how God had used him among the lepers; he unveiled his vision for a leper home. By the service's conclusion, no one was concerned with his age. They merely marveled at his sincerity and commitment.

The following Sunday, Harry joined four other speakers at a missionary convention being held at Highway Tabernacle in Philadelphia. The church was pastored by E. S.

Williams, who had encouraged Harry to come even though he could not guarantee that the cost of his train fare would be reimbursed.

Despite the expense, which, quite possibly, would come out of his own pocket, Harry thanked God for the opportunity and made the long journey. Just prior to stepping to the pulpit to deliver the closing message of the convention, God whispered to Harry's heart to ask for $1,000. Audibly, Harry whispered back, "I thank You, Lord, for $1,000."

Offerings had been raised throughout the week-long convention, and most of the parishioners had already made pledges to specific missionary projects, so Harry rejected the idea of making the request himself.

His sermon was anointed and well-received even though his soft-spoken, gentle style was distinguishable from the rousing, motivational approaches of the other speakers. As E. S. Williams rose to the pulpit, following Harry's presentation, he said, "I feel led by God to take up an offering for Brother Waggoner."

Harry had to bury his eyes in his handkerchief as he saw elderly and young alike reach into their pockets and purses.

The ushers disappeared into the back room with the offering baskets as the service came to a close. Immediately after the benediction, well-wishers gathered around Harry. Meanwhile, Reverend Williams was at the rear of the sanctuary greeting members of his congregation as they filed outside.

"Pastor Williams," an elderly woman said, "may I speak with you in private?"

"Certainly, Sister Brown," he answered, directing her to a clearing in the lobby.

"Pastor, when we took up the offering for tonight's missionary speaker, God spoke to me to give some money I have in a savings account."

"Okay, Sister."

"Well, it's a lot of money. I wanted to know if you thought it was really God because I've been saving this money for a long time."

"Sister Brown, if you think God told you to do it, and you're giving it unto Him, He'll bless you. I'm sure it would be a blessing to Brother Waggoner."

The elderly woman smiled and pulled a check from her purse. "Here, Pastor. I wrote it out but was just afraid to put it in the offering. Please give this $600 toward Reverend Waggoner's work."

"God bless you," Pastor Williams said.

As the slightly bent-over woman hobbled away, a deacon leaned over to whisper in the pastor's ear. "Reverend Williams, here's a check from tonight's offering."

The pastor unfolded the two checks in his hand and made a quick calculation: $1040. To him the handsome sum was especially pleasing, for he wanted to aid Harry in his ministry to the lepers. The offering was even more significant to Harry, for it was as though his Creator was smiling from the heavens, saying, "Well, Harry, if you won't ask for $1,000, I'm going to give it to you anyway . . . because I have called you."

A grateful Harry promptly peered up at the ceiling like a man expecting God to drop his duty papers into his hands.

From Philadelphia, Harry took a train to Newark, New Jersey, to speak at Bethel Church.

"Folks," he said, "God wants us to have compassion like Jesus had. He wants us to be tender. At times when we could not reach the lepers in any other way, the fact that we were moved to tears toward them in their times of awful distress has broken down prejudice. Their hearts have been touched by the sight of our tears, and we've been able to speak to them about Jesus.

"But in the Central Provinces there are many horrible customs. For example, a hideous sickle is used when a baby has colic. The mother or grandmother takes this sickle and heats it under a fire until the tip is white hot. Then she touches the baby's abdomen with the fiery metal as a way of fending off the evil spirits believed to be attacking the child. The scars—if the child survives, that is—are carried with the individual to his or her grave. These people need to witness the love of Jesus, and how He alone can relieve their fears. They needn't resort to sickles and chants and sacrifices."

Harry lowered his head for a moment; fighting tears, he cleared his throat. "These people need to see Jesus' compassion through us. They need Jesus, for without Him we would all be lost. One night after having served in India for over a year, we too felt Jesus' compassion. My wife came to me complaining about a piece of sand in her eye. All I could see was a red spot on her eyelid the size of a small freckle. Four hours later her eye was swollen outside her cheek. She began crying in terror and, since we were quite a distance from a doctor at the time, all I could do was plead for Christ to have compassion on us. I fell to the floor and began to petition heaven. But I was so shaken, I felt as though my prayers weren't reaching the throne of God.

"In desperation, we called for an Indian nurse who used an opium wash to deaden the pain. Then a plaster was applied. But my wife Helen was still in agony, and the swelling had not gone down. Finally, she swiped the substance from her eye and began begging God for relief: 'Whether it will be life or death, I will trust the Lord,' she said. A few minutes later the pain ceased and the swelling began to subside.

"Two weeks later, we received a letter from some dear friends, saying they had been awakened in the middle of the night that very evening and felt led to pray for us. That very night! You see, we've experienced Christ's compassion and know what it can do for the leper who lives in agony. And that's our desire: to return to India to spread the compassion of Jesus Christ to those lepers who have been forsaken and those who have fallen prey to heathenistic superstitions."

Harry turned and found his seat on the platform, almost oblivious to members of the audience who had suddenly risen to their feet in prayer for the people of this foreign land. Even children were praying for the little orphans in Indian villages. Harry had touched them. He had moved the congregation by sharing his heart—not with dynamic gestures and stirring phrases, but rather by exposing them to the compassion God was exhibiting through him.

9
Many Obstacles

To some living in the Ohio countryside, sailing to India was like going to another planet. It was a four-week voyage from New York to Bombay, but for Harry and Helen it was like an endless ride at the state fair. The helm of their ocean liner was manned by the hand of God, and they were determined to enjoy every ocean wave as a blessing from the celestial kingdom. They were going home at last.

The location for the leper home had not been determined, nor had the land been purchased, yet Harry gazed at the Bombay harbor like a man coming to claim an inheritance. The Waggoners felt like the Israelites coming to collect the land God had promised them. This was their destiny.

February 1923, Bombay. A crowd of two hundred natives and missionary workers greeted the Waggoners as they set foot on Indian soil. Well-wishers flung garlands of flowers around their necks before they escorted the Waggoners to a bungalow especially decorated for the occasion. The young couple and their children felt like they had just witnessed a reception worthy of a monarch.

"Why did they give us these?" Willard asked, picking at the strand of orchids hanging on his chest.

Helen said, "They're just happy to see you."

"But I don't know them."

"Yes, but they know we have come to help them. And they just want to be our friends. They want to show their appreciation."

Willard still wore a baffled expression when the last of the welcoming party left the Waggoners' bungalow. The children were busy investigating their new hovel when a knock came to the door. Helen met a short Indian fellow at the doorway. The boy handed her an envelope then vanished like a leaf blown by a gust of wind.

The mysterious letter, addressed to Reverend Harry Waggoner, was from a missionary in Uska Bazar, a two-day journey from Bombay. Miss Bernice Lee, curator of a mission station there, had written to formally invite the Waggoners to consider building their leper home in her vicinity.

Harry prayed the next few evenings with the letter clutched between his hands. Before long he was convinced this letter was a directive from the throne of God. Several weeks later, Harry loaded the family onto a train for the beautiful trek to Uska Bazar.

Miss Lee was waiting as they deboarded in March 1923. She was a round-faced woman, on the heels of forty, donning the clothes of a much older woman. Her bungalow was not large enough to comfortably house an entire family. With the Waggoners moving in for an extended stay, Harry knew the bungalow had to be enlarged.

Harry immediately ordered bricks and other materials, which native workers transported to the job site. With the help of a sizable work crew, the missionary quarters were swiftly renovated. But Harry had not traveled such a great distance to construct just an addition to missionary quarters. He had higher aspirations: to build a home for lepers.

With high expectations he set out to purchase land for the missionary-leper home. The venture proved to be tearfully depressing, however. Each potential parcel of land toyed with Harry's hopes, his dreams dancing between optimism and defeat. But every time Harry felt like leaving Uska Bazar, the sights and sounds of these leprous outcasts gave him courage to continue his search for land.

Harry discovered that a wealthy landowner had threatened to harm anyone selling land to the missionary. The man, a Hindu named Mangal Prashad, had actively undermined Harry's plans for a leper home. No one would sell land for fear of inciting the community leader's wrath. Besides Prashad's injunction, the purchase of land was made more difficult, at times, by the reality that each plot of land had multiple owners. Even the deputy magistrates found it difficult to determine all the rightful owners of properties in this region of misshaped superstitions and demon worship.

Despite the setbacks, Harry would not surrender to the enemy. Night after night, he joined hands with Helen and Bernice and prayed for God's intervention.

Several months passed, and still no land had been freed from the enemy's grasp. The missionaries were further concerned: they lacked the monies to purchase the land if indeed they found a plot.

An uninterrupted blue sky hovered over Uska Bazar when Harry ambled back to the bungalow after an unfruitful afternoon of seeking property. Two men were waiting for him when he arrived. One's sideburn's were speckled with gray; the other so youthful he did not shave.

Speaking Hindi, the younger man asked, "Are you Harry Waggoner?"

"Yes. How may I help you?"

The older man stepped forward. "We have some property to sell. The woman inside told us to wait."

"Thank you for waiting. How much property do you have, and where is it located?" he asked.

By this time Harry had learned not to become too excited with prospective real estate.

"We will show you," the man said, shaking like a drug addict. Harry later discovered the man was an avid gambler and alcoholic.

"Aren't you concerned about what Prashad will say?"

"We aren't afraid of him. Come!"

With a contradiction of emotions, Harry followed the men two miles down a dirt road to a stretch of land, estimated at five and one-half acres, just twenty miles from the Nepal border. The land, near the village Katka, had obviously been left untended. It was overgrown with low vegetation, but not to the point that it would require great expense for clearing. The elevation of the property kept it safe from flooding, yet it was suitable for the type of structures Harry wanted to build.

Harry was ecstatic over the prospect of obtaining the land, yet he harnessed his optimism. He had one major obstacle to hurdle: he had no money, and he knew the sellers would want to be paid in cash. Harry grew convinced this was the property God had ordained, but he needed heavenly direction to know how to pay for it.

Harry said, "I am interested, but I need several days to make a decision."

The men were noticeably upset over the delay but threw up their arms and agreed to wait.

When dawn broke on Wednesday morning, Harry had been agonizing in prayer all night, uttering phrases of desperation better suited for a man about to be hanged. "Father," he prayed, "if You want us to remain here, if this is the land You have for us, please speak to me. Please show me by sending us twenty-five cents in today's mail. Then I'll know You'll provide the money we need."

Foreign mail usually arrived on Sunday afternoons, but that day a letter from England mysteriously arrived with the local mail. As he opened the envelope a check fluttered to the floor. Lifting it to his eyes, he could hardly believe the amount made out in his name: 250 English pounds, or $1,250. Harry lowered his head and wept, too overwhelmed to shout for joy. For Harry, this was another sign that he was where God wanted him.

It was minutes before he could even read the letter. For many years, an English woman had been saving money for a leper home. Many times she was tempted to donate the funds to other worthy causes, but she felt checked each time. She heard of the Uska Bazar project when a friend read to her a letter from Stanley Frodsham, editor of the Assemblies of God *Pentecostal Evangel.* Immediately, the woman knew this was the ministry to which she was to contribute.

"Helen!" he screamed. "Helen, come here! You will not believe this. Helen, hurry!"

She ran inside from a clothesline strung along the side of the bungalow, a pair of shirts in her hands.

"What is it?" she asked.

"God has answered our prayer," he said, handing her the check.

"Dear Lord Jesus, thank you!" she declared.

The couple embraced.

"What's all the excitement?" Bernice inquired, stepping through the door.

Helen passed her the check. "This was sent to buy the land."

Bernice's face swelled as she read the zeros. "God has provided!" she announced, as though she knew He would. "God has called you here."

Helen gave her friend a hug then took another lasting look at the check.

Even with the funds in hand, Harry was having unforeseen difficulty prying loose the property God promised. The temptation to leave the area for another site languished, yet

Harry would not allow himself to be misdirected. He knew God brought him to Uska Bazar for a purpose.

Harry was quite leery of the two men who had shown him the property. Their word meant nothing, as Harry soon discovered, for they owned only a small share of the property. If the parcel was to be sold, Harry would have to come to an agreement with everyone claiming the land. He spent entire afternoons bargaining with these men and their many partners. The two men who originally proposed the transaction were anxious to get the deal settled. They were willing to ignore laws and proper deed transfer procedures, perhaps because they knew this would allow them to blackmail Harry later. But God gave the missionary wisdom. Harry required the landowners to accompany him on a fifteen mile trip to the courthouse in Bansi where they could properly register the transfer. Again the men bickered, complaining about the legal arrangement.

They even threatened to cancel the deal.

"Wait!" Harry shouted as the men rose to their feet to leave the courthouse without signing the papers. "What will you tell the other owners of the land? They are expecting their money."

The two men looked at one another and returned to their chairs, again complaining, demanding more money for their property.

On September 11, 1923, the deal was finalized.

Harry walked into the bungalow the following afternoon with a grandiose smile. "Helen! Bernice! It's all ours!" he declared.

Helen hugged Harry and Bernice shouted, "Hallelujah!"

Little Beatrice hopped into the living room with Almeta at her heels. Helen hugged them as well.

"Why are you so happy, Mother?" Beatrice asked.

"We have land to build us a home and a home for the lepers."

Beatrice clapped and grinned. Almeta and the other children cheered. Then Harry brought a level sobriety to the scene. "Let's thank God," he said. The group gathered in a circle, held hands, and joined in as Bernice prayed, "Thank you, Father, for sending me a family . . . ." With that utterance, Bernice broke into tears, the prayer ended, and the hugs reconvened.

One morning, a man yelled from outside the bungalow. "Sahib, Sahib!"

Harry came to the door and started down the steps to meet the man.

"Stop, Sahib," he said in his Hindi tongue. "I am a leper."

Despite the warning, Harry drew closer.

"Sahib, I am a leper. You mustn't come near me."

"Yes, I know. How may I help you?"

"The lepers in the countryside say you have come to build a home for us. Can this be true?"

"That is true. Jesus, the Man who healed lepers, has sent me to this place."

"Who is this Jesus you speak of?"

"What is your name, sir?" Harry asked.

"Khushi."

"Khushi, Jesus is God's Son who came to earth many years ago. He healed lepers, blind men, and even some who could not walk. He sacrificed His life so you, Khushi, could live, and He sent me to build for you a home of your very own."

"What must I do to repay this Jesus?"

"He only asks that you believe He is the only true God."

The Hindu leper promptly backed away, saying, "The gods would not approve of this."

Harry, sensing Khushi's trepidation, said, "Jesus will give you a home. Then you will see how kind and compassionate and powerful He is."

"Sahib, since my disease, I have no home."

"I know, Khushi, but Jesus has sent me to be your friend and to give you a home."

"When will I have a home, Sahib?"

"Very soon. God is preparing the land as we speak."

The vile face of this man contorted as if to smile. Harry could only grin as he watched the leper saunter away with a sense of pride and hope.

A few days later, a much younger man visited Harry. He too had heard of the Waggoners' plans to build a home. He had a large ulcer on his leg that had not been cleansed in many weeks. Bernice raced to his aid like a medic in a battlefield. After cleansing his wound and giving it a dressing, she answered his inquiries about a leper home. Within days, the man's sore began to greatly improve, and thus word spread throughout the countryside of the white man's healing power. Other lepers began making the arduous journey to the bungalow in search of medical attention.

A woman who had cut her hand with a sickle also came. The entire back of her hand, from her wrist to her fingers, was one bloody mass. Infection had set in. The skin was discolored. Harry and Bernice feared she might lose her hand. Nevertheless, they treated her morning after morning, all the while praying God would chastise the infection.

As news of the woman's recovery circulated, more than lepers began coming to the missionaries for medical attention. Morning after morning, as many as two hundred natives lined up outside their bungalow. Harry, Helen, and Bernice knew very little about medicine other than standard precautionary measures such as cleansing wounds, treating them with disinfectant, and applying bandages. In many cases that was all they needed to bring healing to wounds and illnesses.

"Thank you," each said in their native tongue. Bernice responded, "Don't thank us. Thank the one true God."

The visits of such needy men and women had actually caused Harry to grow more impatient with Indian officials and red tape. He had witnessed how providing villagers with medical care had served to open the doors to their hearts, and, with each passing day, more lepers were winding their way closer to eternity. We could help more lepers and villagers, Harry thought, if we just could scale the legal barriers and build the leper home. Provincial leaders, however, had ruled that no construction could begin until all disputes were settled surrounding the real estate.

Ultimately, a lawsuit was brought against Harry regarding the property's boundary lines.

Without witnesses in his defense, and with many misgivings, Harry went to court. Fortunately, a prominent, well-versed Hindu, Kanhaiya Pare, served as Harry's counsel. Pare was of the Brahmin caste. He wore nice clothing and lived in a large house with a walled-in courtyard. Yet with all his wealth and status, and much to lose, Pare continually came to the defense of missionaries. Before Harry's arrival in Uska Bazar, Pare had fended off an unruly mob threatening to harm Bernice and her co-workers. He put himself in front of the would-be attackers, saying, "Come closer and you will have to deal with me." Now, in Harry's defense, he was ready to make that same stand.

A Hindu attorney represented the group attempting to confiscate the land Harry had purchased. The well-dressed, copper-skinned lawyer declared, "This man, Harry Waggoner, is guilty of stealing land from Indian citizens. He is a thief who has come here to take advantage of our people."

The young missionary shook his head while the caustic attorney made his accusations. Pare sat without expression, as if he had witnessed his opponent's fiery tirades before.

The assault continued for ten minutes. "Mr. Waggoner is guilty, I tell you. He knowingly took land that he was not entitled to. He says he wants to build a leper home. No, he has come here to bring profit to himself. Lepers can take care of themselves. They don't need a white man's help. They don't need the white man's God."

Pare strode to the front of the court room and said calmly, "Your Honor, these accusations are unfounded. There is no proof, and I ask that this case be dropped so Mr. Waggoner can proceed with building his home for lepers."

The judge peered into Harry's pupils before announcing his decision. The missionary was praying silently as the judge contemplated his response.

"The court rules in favor of Mr. Waggoner," the judge said.

Slamming his notepad onto the table, the belligerent attorney cast a sneer at Harry.

With a slight nod of the head, Harry smiled; he could not contain his relief and satisfaction. Moreover, he smiled because he could almost hear the heavenly hosts celebrating the outcome with shouts of victory.

Some months later, once the building of the leper home was underway, Harry learned the opposing attorney had been stricken with leprosy. And to himself, the missionary repeated, "It's dangerous to curse the living God."

10
Heartbroken

Once the lawsuit was thrown out of court, it was not long before the foundations were in place for a row of leper homes and living quarters for the missionaries. Once again, God had miraculously provided the funds for construction. When the donor from England learned the property had been purchased on September 11—her deceased child's birthday—the woman sent a sizable contribution in her daughter's memory. Her check for 750 English pounds or $3,750 was enough to complete the first stage of Harry's master plan.

Months passed, and Harry was brimming with smiles. His vision was materializing before his eyes, like a child watching his father build him a plastic model.

Joy turned to heartache, however, one ordinary afternoon. Margaret, their fifth child, had been born in March 1924, but had been sick with a slight case of whooping cough.

"Harry! Harry!" Helen yelled from the bungalow to the brick pile Harry was leaning against.

Even from that distance, Harry could see she was terribly upset. He came running.

Meanwhile, Helen raced back to Margaret's crib. Harry trailed.

"She's not breathing!" Helen cried.

Harry placed his hand on the baby's head and prayed. "Dear God, save my daughter. Please!"

Seconds later, he knew it was over. His little girl was dead.

Helen ran from the room. Harry fell into a chair and wept, helplessly asking, "Why, God?"

"Daddy!" Beatrice hollered while skipping into Margaret's room. "What . . . ?"

Her sentence was cut short by the sight of her father placing Margaret into a box lined with white cloth. The sound of her father hammering nails into the lid of the coffin sent Beatrice running from the room. Helen and the other children also heard the incessant banging. Each nail reiterated the finality of the moment. Willard wrapped his arm around his mother's waist—much like Harry would have had he been by her side. But even the loving arms of a child could not temper her grief. India had taken two of her most precious possessions.

That afternoon, the Waggoners buried Margaret behind the chapel located across the road from the bungalow. The family encircled the gravesite, tears dripping onto the soil they had grown to love. Behind them stood a group of native workers. And in the distance a trio of lepers observed the simple ceremony.

As Harry concluded his prayer, with Helen under his arm, he focused his eyes on the three lepers. He could not tell who they were or why they had come to the funeral. As he watched them struggle to sit on their haunches, Harry realized he could not allow the enemy's attacks on him and his family to dissuade him from fulfilling his vow to help the lepers. The building of the leper home had to proceed on schedule. With a renewed sense of determination, Harry grabbed his shovel at daybreak and plunged it into the ground. It was his way of burying his grief, refocusing his attention on his task, and sending a message to the enemy that he would not be derailed from God's plan.

11
Edith and Bernice

Edith Dutton's arrival was like that of an angel—bearing a stethoscope—swooping down on the leper compound. She was a registered nurse who came to Uska Bazar to treat the many disorders she had heard about in Bible school.

"Edith, it's important that you're extremely careful when you begin treating the natives," Harry advised. "Helen and I and Bernice have been a little too careless. Please take as many precautions as you need to."

"Yes, I understand," she smiled, nodding her brunette head.

Harry and Helen instructed their children not to touch the lepers. They had even refrained from letting them have a pet for fear the disease might spread through the animal. And, for the most part, the children had been conscious of their parents' warnings.

Edith, on the other hand, did not heed Harry's instructions. Her first day on the job she began touching lepers without wearing gloves.

"Edith," Harry scorned, "you must be careful."

"God will protect me," the attractive woman answered. "There are just too many who need immediate treatment to be concerned with anything else."

Harry wagged his head in frustration, though grateful God had sent him a selfless, hardworking associate. He only hoped she would survive the long lines of patients coming from surrounding villages. Even the Waggoner children had to work to keep up with the stream of ill natives. The older children spent part of their days grinding medicine in a ceramic bowl while the adults assisted Edith with applying salve and bandaging wounds.

Edith worked from dawn to dusk, tirelessly treating the sick until each received proper care. Sometimes she worked well into the night, occasionally having to pull an abscessed tooth or set a broken bone without anesthesia. In those instances the howling of a native echoed through the trees like the sound of an animal caught in the thicket.

The nearest hospital was forty miles away. Most natives did not have the money to pay physician's fees anyway, so the local inhabitants viewed Edith's "magic" as a blessing from the gods.

Although Harry had no medical training other than what he had learned in Baitalpur, he found himself filling the shoes of a physician more often than he liked. Prior to Edith's arrival, Harry was called on to administer more than first aid. One afternoon, in particular, a worker came sprinting to where Harry was tutoring a group of natives in the art of making bricks.

"Sahib, you must come. Gopal needs you."

Running back to where the elderly leper lay, Harry grimaced as he examined the man's toes. It had all the appearances of gangrene.

"Sahib," the man begged, "take my leg if you must, but let me live."

Harry knew the hospital was too far away, so either he had to amputate or let his friend die.

"Help me! Do what you must!" the man cried in agony.

Harry was torn, knowing he was not trained for such an operation, yet realizing he did not have much choice in the matter. After a few moments of indecision, Harry turned to the native worker who had sought him in the fields.

He ordered, "Start a fire and put a saw through the flame until it is red hot. Go!"

Having witnessed amputations in Baitalpur, Harry had seen men die on the operating table even though the procedure was being administered by a doctor. He feared the same might happen, that the man's blood might be on his hands, but he knew he had to try. The fiery blade pierced the man's flesh like a knife through a baked ham until it hit bone. Without the luxury of a local anesthesia, the man's face gyrated uncontrollably. His hands clutched two leper assistants as Harry began sawing into the bone. Blood vessels were now visible in the man's arms, for the leprous man was squeezing with all his might. Then with a tornado's blast, he exhaled and began screaming hysterically. Harry wanted to stop this torture, but he knew it was too late.

When it was finally over, Harry applied the proper bandages. As the bleeding stopped, the missionary sighed deeply, thanking God for directing his hand. Now that Edith was there, Harry hoped he would never have to endure such an ordeal again. Little did he know his medical feats had only begun.

Harry determined that Edith, Bernice, and Margaret Flint, a third unmarried missionary who had joined the team, were deserving of more suitable accommodations. They could find no solitude living in their bungalow, which was desperately in need of repair. During the rainy season they woke up with wind penetrating the walls and water dripping through a sagging roof onto their blankets.

Harry was also unhappy that, after the long hours, the three women were forced to ride bicycles to and from the colony—sometimes after the sun had subsided.

Because of A. G. Ward's fundraising efforts, it was not long before new living quarters for the three women were completed in the compound. Thereafter, they were noticeably more comfortable—if there was such a feeling in India when one works sixteen-hour days. Their house had two rooms, a front and back veranda, a small pantry, and a kitchen that was separated from the rest of the house to reduce heat.

Bernice, who had lived in the bungalow for years, was like a child as she bounced from room to room in her new dwelling. "Thank you, Father," she said repeatedly, her hands clasped together below her chin. She giggled as though she inherited a mansion rather than the humble nest that it was.

About the time the women moved onto the compound, the Waggoner's three eldest children were sent off to boarding school. Harry and Helen begrudged the day their children were to leave, for it signified the beginning of nine months of separation. Helen cried as Willard, Donald, and Beatrice boarded the train for school in the Himalaya Mountains.

"They'll be fine," Harry decreed, patting her hand.

"I know. I'll just miss them; that's all."

"Well, the time will go fast, but I'll miss them too."

Beatrice's tear-stained face smudged against the inside of the train's glass window as Donald and Willard stared and waved farewell. Their parents waved back, shielding their own grief with imitation smiles.

Several weeks later, the missionary couple received a letter from Willard with news that Donald had become homesick and ran into the woods. They had found him sitting on a tree stump, crying. Before Helen read the last paragraph of Willard's letter, she found herself wanting to board a train to come to Donald's aid.

Unfortunately, there was far too much work to do and no extra funds for such a costly trip. All she could do was worry, cry, and pray. And that she did until she drifted to sleep that evening.

"I'm so thankful that Doris and Almeta are with us," Helen said to herself, "and that we have another on the way. What would I do without their joyful faces around here?"

Doris took a special liking to Bernice. The veteran missionary often invited the little blonde-headed youngster to ride with her on the oxcart when she visited outlying villages. And every time the cart rolled through a dip in the dirt road, Doris' face exuded a chuckle.

"Bouncey," Bernice said in a childish tongue, prompting Doris to laugh some more. For her it was like an amusement park ride. For Bernice, the journey merely jostled her bones.

So it was with feelings of grandeur that Bernice welcomed a new Ford Model T—a gift from friends in the States. The four-seat convertible, equipped with a crank starter, was the first car seen in the area. Villagers came from miles around to catch a glimpse of this oxless cart.

The vehicle made it easier for Bernice and others to reach distant villages in need of the gospel. For Doris and the other children, it proved to be more exhilarating than riding the oxcart. As the motorized vehicle peaked at twenty-five miles per hour, the children poked their heads out the window and allowed the air to slap against their faces, which provided temporary relief from the heat.

Aunty Lee, as she was affectionately called, was only concerned with what the automobile might do to enhance their efforts in reaching natives with the gospel. The red-haired woman knew that because this society had relegated many women—especially in the obscure villages—to slaves and had segregated them from the men, it would take a woman to reach a woman.

To the natives, Bernice was known as "Mamajee," meaning the "mother of many." Because she did not have children of her own, that tag pleased her more than she cared to let on. She treated the Waggoner kids as though they were her own, telling them stories of the great Chicago revival and the miracles she had seen.

More than her stories, though, it was her sacrifice, faith, and courage that marveled the children. When they crawled out of their cots in the early morning hours to visit the portable toilet stationed on the porch, they saw a lantern lit in her room. The missionaries placed lanterns around the latrine so snakes would stay away. As the children sat on the porch, still conscious of snakes, they listened to Bernice tearfully mention their names in her prayers. She woke every morning at four o'clock to spend time alone with God.

Bernice took her faith seriously, but she was not so solemn or reverent that she could not appreciate a good joke or prank. On one occasion, when it was too hot to eat inside, the family gathered for dinner in the front yard. Harry had decided to test Bernice's sense of humor. He asked an employee to carve a piece of wood so it resembled a chicken leg. Then Harry had the leg rolled in flower, fried, and placed on the dinner table. Bernice had a fetish for chicken, especially the leg portion. As was the custom, everyone refrained from eating the legs. Bernice quickly snatched the imitation leg. Her first nibble sounded like someone trying to bite into the pit of a peach.

It took her a few moments to figure out what had happened, then without expression, she heaved the piece of wood across the yard at an innocent-looking Harry. He ducked and the missile collided with the dirt. Everyone convulsed with laughter; even the natives were clapping.

"Okay, Harry Waggoner, I'll get you for this," she said, smirking beneath a raised fist.

12
Con Artists and Thieves

Before all the leper homes were completed, news of the facility had spread among the legions of lepers. They heard rumors that white men and women had come to treat them and give them food so that begging no longer had to be their unenviable lot.

Some of the lepers who traveled many miles had to live under trees and in ditches until more homes were completed. Many took up residence surrounding a large banyan tree between Uska and the compound. There they congregated under the shade, begging for food and money from passing strangers.

The lepers kept a watchful eye on the progress of the complex. Once the homes were finished, they knew Harry would be at the entrance to welcome them into their Disneyland, the place of refuge he had slaved to build. The two rows of leper homes were not ordinary dormitories. Each facility housed two lepers, either two men or husband and wife. Each had its own cooking area and a plot for a small garden. Many married couples had been separated from each other or from their children because of leprosy. Harry set out to restore their self-respect and a chance at a normal way of life by giving them a home.

The facility began to take shape. Everyday, for at least a few minutes, Harry removed his pith helmet, wiped his brow, then strolled around the complex to admire God's handiwork. He gazed at the last rays of the sunset touching the tops of the grand old Himalayas in the distance. Just below the white peaks, he could see the dark outline of the lower hills of Nepal. Stretching far in the distance, in every direction, the restful green of waving wheat appealed to his eye. And along the roadway, carts were being drawn by slow-moving oxen, followed by a number of travelers winding their way homeward. It was all so beautiful and serene, yet nothing matched the beauty of the leper complex.

"Yes," he proclaimed, as though standing on holy ground, "God is good. We're making progress."

Youthful workers, who spoke only Hindi, looked up at him without a shred of understanding and smiled. They did not know the meaning of his words; they just knew their employer was happy.

With the two missionary bungalows and a chapel in place, and several more leper homes near completion, Harry and his makeshift work crew began drawing plans for an addition to the facility. Harry and Helen wanted a separate building for widowed and single women—the zenana—which would be surrounded by a high wall to ensure their privacy. Later, an orphanage and a residence for the workers would be constructed. The orphanage was occupied by the "clean" children of lepers and youngsters from neighboring villages who were destitute or without parents.

Under the Florida-like sun, Harry determined to plant as many trees as he could afford: banana, mango, palm, and guava. To ensure the trees would be healthy and laden with fruit, Harry buried dead animals under the trees, claiming they served as rich fertilizer. Eventually, he was able to purchase an additional two acres where he grew rice, sweet peas, and other vegetables.

The buildings, made of both sun-dried and kilned brick, were white with red-tiled roofs. The facility was like a colonial plantation or Pukka (permanent buildings) in the middle of agricultural terrain. No one took more pride in its appearance than Harry. He believed the lepers deserved the finest. When guests rode through the archway past the missionary bungalows, down the road running north and south that separated the cottages from the chapel, they were pleasantly surprised by its immaculate appearance. Because the monsoon often took its toll, Harry made sure the walls were whitewashed each year. He also demanded that the groundskeepers keep the paths and yards tidy. "This belongs to God, and He deserves that it look its best," Harry preached to his workers.

The surrounding villages, comprised of mostly farmers, ranged between 200 and 1,000 inhabitants. Their hovels, for the most part, were made of thatch roofs and dirt floors. The nearest village, Katka, was only one-half mile from the leper home. Harry maintained popularity among the villagers because he was willing to assume responsibility for the community's orphans and lepers. Moreover, they were grateful for the free medical attention he awarded in the dispensary.

Uska Bazar, the largest village in the vicinity, boasted over 2,000 inhabitants. It was a popular resting place for lepers, beggars, and vagabonds. Upon learning of the home, lepers often detoured from Uska Bazar to interrogate the peculiar missionary who left America to live in a land with leprosy.

Although the leper homes were often filled, Harry was constantly faced with a decision: whether to allow more lepers to enter the compound even though it might require that some sleep on a porch or floor.

Harry said to one elderly leper, "I wish I could offer you a roof over your head, but there is no room available."

The man, nearly sixty, cupped his hands together, begging, "Please, Sahib, I will be your slave. I do not need a roof; just a home."

Recognizing the man's leprosy was the variety that merely discolors the skin with white splotches, Harry said, "I'm sorry; we have no room."

Tears formed in the man's eyes. Harry felt the spears of guilt piercing his side as he looked away. To himself, he said, "Who am I to play God? Surely this man is old and needs Christ, but there are so many like him. What can I do? There are others who are in worse condition."

The man, refusing to leave, fell prostrate at Harry's feet.

With moisture collecting on his face, Harry ordered the man to stand. Then, looking him in the eye, Harry said, "I wish I could give you all you need, but I cannot. Here, take this money and buy food. Forgive me. Forgive me."

The following day, another man struggled to the gate. He too was searching for solitude, but his condition was far worse: open sores, labored breathing, and the suffocating stench of decaying flesh.

"Can you walk?" Harry asked, his face red from working near the brick kiln.

The man nodded his head as he trailed Harry to Edith's stable. After treating the man, Harry made an inquiry of his sad plight, then with a sense of incongruity, he offered *this* man a veranda to sleep on.

The missionary had learned that some lepers were merely con artists, systematically wandering from missionary to missionary, reaping the rewards of their kindness: taking food, blankets, and money, then leaving in the middle of the evening for another mission to repeat the same scheme. In Calcutta, "professional" lepers hired by businessmen have been known to deceive Westerners into emptying their wallets. The lepers then surrender a percentage from their take to their pimp-like employers.

During the first month the facility was opened, a man came dressed as a sadhu, a holy man. He had a long beard and shoulder-length hair that was matted with cow dung and ashes. Wearing only a loin cloth, the man declared his desire to accept Christ, but more emphatically, he pleaded for Harry's help. He wanted food, lodging, and money.

Sensing the man was insincere, Harry sent the visitor on his way. Many of these beggars or con men had been baptized a dozen times. And Harry was not in the mood for another charade.

A year later the same man returned, wearing a silk-like suit and an expensive shirt. He was also carrying a flashlight—a real status symbol in those days. When Harry recognized the man's face, he threw back his head and erupted with laughter. Many of the workers gathered around, their eyes glaring with bewilderment.

Harry said, "You were here once before. You came posing as a desperate man. Why have you returned?"

The con artist jumped from his chair on the veranda and suddenly exhaled as though the air had been knocked from his lungs.

"Go quickly or I will turn you over to the authorities!" Harry snapped, pointing toward the front gate.

Without a word, the man collected his belongings and swiftly retreated.

When Harry turned to order the men back to work, he was met with sets of smiling teeth, as if to say, "Pastor, you are a wise man."

Although Harry was intent on leading the lepers to a saving knowledge of Christ, he did not require them to attend chapel services. Because of the strong Hindu and

Muslim influence, Harry believed it was wise for them to come to chapel services on their own volition. Still, Helen played the reed organ and Harry preached to a capacity crowd each Sunday.

While the services were in progress, some, who were afraid to enter the building, listened from the path outside the chapel. One by one, they gained the courage to step inside and walk to the podium to accept Christ as their personal Savior.

A group of devout Muslims chanting to Allah or Hindus celebrating one of their many goddess festivals occasionally interrupted their services. Hindu parades stretched from village to village, the participants garbed in colorful costumes, offering pujas (prayers) to their respective gods.

Because there was neither electricity nor adequate lighting, church services were conducted during the day. The chapel, which was configured in the shape of a cross, divided the leper men and women by a center aisle; the clean men and women were segregated on the wings.

One Sunday, a teenage boy virtually crawled into the compound. Harry approached the boy who, sitting on his haunches, had braced himself against a wall.

"Won't you join us in the chapel?" Harry asked.

The young man stared at the ground.

"Will you join us?" Harry repeated.

"I do not walk," the boy said, his eyes still fixed on the dirt.

"Come; we'll carry you."

"I do not wish to leave."

Harry never sought to impose Christ upon sinners. Rather, he endeavored to expose them to the love of Christ so they could see the superiority of the Christian life and choose for themselves. Deciding not to violate his convictions, Harry dashed off to preach another sermon while the teenager lingered behind.

It was unusual for the minister to stop and talk to anyone before a Sunday service. Ordinarily, he awoke at dawn on Sundays, withdrew to a room, and sought God in prayer. No one saw or spoke to him until he walked down the center aisle to deliver the message God had inspired him to preach.

Just before he was to preach this particular Sunday, Harry excused himself abruptly. He walked out the side door back into the quad area where the lad had been sitting. The natives stirred in their wooden stools, wondering what had caused their pastor's sudden departure.

Soon Harry's voice boomed above the chatter emanating from the chapel.

"Young man, you lied to me and are stealing from God!"

"Leave me alone!" the boy spit, turning to run away.

Harry grabbed the teenager's arm—the arm that held kitchen utensils and coins pilfered from the homes.

"This is wrong!" Harry said, raising his voice to an infrequent pitch. "Do you understand? You lied to me! You said you couldn't walk. Now look at you. You came here to steal."

The young man, his eyes glazed with fury, swung his fist from his waist and connected with Harry's shoulder, causing the missionary to lose his grasp.

Instinctively, Harry kicked the boy in the shin with his congregation looking on.

In haste, the boy fled the compound, leaving his spoils in his wake.

As though nothing had happened, Harry returned to the pulpit and began his sermon. It hurt to have his kindness and trust betrayed. His own fit of rage also troubled him. Yet, unbeknownst to the meek preacher, this episode gained him supreme respect among his parishioners. Indian philosophy states, "A man must do what he must do to stand for truth and honesty." Harry learned this lesson many times over in the days ahead, although he vowed not to become as cynical as some missionaries—refusing to trust anyone.

Years later some would say it was perhaps this desire to bestow trust in his fellow man that cost him his dream.

13
Glorious Conversions

Raghunath was a friendly Hindu leper who openly shared his disbelief in the Christian religion. To his credit, though, he did not allow that to interfere with his love for Harry, Helen, and their children. He often told the Caucasian family the gods were pleased by their generosity and sacrifice.

Harry recognized Raghunath's commitment to his faith and, in private, told Helen that one day the leper would have the same zeal for Jesus Christ. But Raghunath was stubborn, showing no signs of withdrawing his opposition to the concept of a savior. He was one of the few lepers who was educated and could read, so he had come to the mission with a basic understanding of Christ's teachings.

Like most lepers, he had his own desperate story. He contracted leprosy at age twenty-four after launching a successful mercantile business. Despite being ridiculed by his community as a "recipient of the gods' wrath," he worked for eight years.

In search of a healing, Raghunath squandered his estate, traveling from one holy man to another. He even bathed in the Ganges River in hope of being cured. But nowhere in the course of his seven-year nomadic journey did he find relief from the dreaded disease. Nonetheless, he remained steadfast in his Hindu beliefs. That same loyalty convinced Harry that Raghunath would make a very fine Christian.

An Englishman had informed Raghunath of the mission, and since the leper was penniless, he had come there to spend his remaining years.

Raghunath was fortunate in one sense: his face was not too distorted. His feet, though, were undergoing rapid deterioration. To make it possible for him to walk on crutches, rubber tire treads were wrapped around his feet, which were now nothing more than fatty stumps. Later, even that became too painful and difficult, so Harry's children pulled him around in their red wagon.

He loved children, and the affection was mutual. They enjoyed watching Raghunath do his acrobatic stunts: handstands, somersaults, and more. In exchange for his entertainment, the Waggoner children gave him Indian candy. When his eyes fell on a chocolate bar, he would do any trick they requested. The old man also enjoyed Harry's sermonettes. He listened respectfully as the missionary told him one biblical story followed by another. Harry slowly saw his friend wilting.

"Would you like to accept Christ, Raghunath?" Harry asked, realizing that a water baptism service was to be held the following week in the river. The leper rubbed his mustache as if selecting his words cautiously.

"Sahibjee," he said, pointing to a wheat field, "even though there are full heads of wheat on the stalks, it would be ruinous to cut the wheat now when it is three weeks away. My heart is like that wheat field; I'll let you know when it is ripe."

Harry smiled, closed his eyes, and nodded his head, thinking it was only a matter of time.

Naomi was born in a village three miles from the leper home. At the age of twelve she was married, and, shortly thereafter, she began having children. After the birth of her third child, Naomi lost feeling in one of her fingers. Then the paralysis spread to her feet and slowly throughout her other appendages. Although she was a mere twenty-four years of age, she had trouble walking.

Upon hearing of her leprous fate, the villagers kept their distance from Naomi. When her husband died, she was nudged outside the village altogether. She and her three children stayed with her father even though Harry and Bernice had invited her to live in the colony, where she could be near her children without endangering them. Furthermore, she feared what her relatives would do if she embraced the white man's faith. Finally, shredding her apprehensions about entering what she deemed a Christian commune, Naomi and her children took up residence on the mission grounds.

Despite her affiliation to Hinduism, Naomi listened week after week for two years to Harry's sermons.

"Do you believe in Jesus?" Harry asked Naomi.

"Yes, Sahib," she said.

"Do you believe He died for your sins?"

"Yes, Sahib."

"Then do you wish to take water baptism?"

Her hesitation told Harry that Naomi had not fully accepted Christ as her Savior. Water baptism was a sure sign that Hindus had rejected their faith.

She said awkwardly, "I am not ready now."

One morning, as the first piercing ray of light flashed on the horizon, Naomi hobbled to the Waggoners' veranda. "Sahib!" she hollered. "Sahib! This is Naomi."

Harry stumbled out of bed into the grey morning light, his hair in disarray. "Yes, Naomi. What is it?" he slurred.

"God spoke to me in my sleep. I talked to Him. He wants me to take baptism."

Harry wasn't sure what to make of her claims, but to her it was real. He was not about to let this opportunity pass.

"Wait where you are," he said. "We'll go to the river right now."

The woman brought her wrapped hands to her forehead as if to acknowledge his command.

By the time Harry returned to her side, lanterns were popping on across the compound and heads were poking out windows. Within minutes, an explanation for the disturbance had hummed throughout the mission, and workers and lepers followed Harry and Naomi to the river to witness the momentous occasion.

Gunnu Singh, a white-haired man, lived on his haunches—at least that's how it appeared. He spent his afternoons in the same position against the same wooden pole. He had come to the colony with his hands looking well-manicured for a leper, but as the months wore on they began to resemble the paws of a dog. Whenever his beard itched, he rubbed his chin against his chest and made purring noises.

Gunnu was one of the lepers who seemed to be on the verge of making a decision for Christ. But one night, with the urging of another leper, Gunnu fled the mission. Perhaps he was afraid that his affection for God was growing, or maybe he was just influenced by his peers, but Gunnu was gone. Harry was heartbroken.

"Leave me alone for a while, please," Harry said meekly to Helen and Willard. "I need to seek God on Gunnu's behalf. God wants him to come back here."

Two days later, just before Harry was to conduct a baptismal service, whispers of Gunnu's return filtered through the camp. Harry was tempted to give his friend a warm embrace, as if he were "the prodigal," when the two met face to face.

"Why did you leave? Where did you go?" Harry barked.

Gunnu let his eyes sag shamefully. "I leave . . . ."

Harry could see by his friend's embarrassment it was unwise to press for an explanation.

"Don't worry, Gunnu. We're just glad you're back."

Gunnu lifted his chin and grinned.

Following Harry to the river, Gunnu wasted little time ripping off the Hindu charms dangling from his neck and confessing his faith in the one true God. With one swoop, he then cut off the lock of hair denoting his faith in Hinduism and watched it as it floated downstream.

Gokul had made his living as a cook but by the time he arrived at the leper home, he was virtually an invalid. Prostrating himself under the archway at the entrance to the mission, he waited patiently for someone to come to his rescue. Harry, summoned by a native worker, found Gokul, this pitiful man, lying in his own vomit. Large worms had entered his nose and worked their way up into his head. Hundreds of worms were removed over the course of three hours. Gokul was then bathed and offered food; but the Hindu refused the food because it had been prepared by Christian hands.

The following morning, Gokul left the facility. Harry studied the leper's back as he departed, wondering if the hours of medical attention had done anything to tear down the man's prejudices against the Christian faith.

To Harry's delight, with regularity thereafter, Gokul could be seen limping down the dirt road toward the mission. He was growing attached to the care and the people.

One afternoon, Harry invited Gokul to take a walk under a row of shade trees. It was an awkward sight: one man walking so stately, the other dragging his feet like a polio victim.

"Gokul," Harry asked, "where do you come from?"

"Uska."

"Are you a Hindu?"

"Yes, Sahib."

"How long have you been a leper?"

"Ten years."

"I want you to know, Gokul, that I have been praying to my God for you."

"Thank you, but that is unnecessary. I have seen a sadhu, and I have obeyed him. He told me to take bark from the neem tree and the snake-poisoned roots of one of the forest trees and put them in vessels of water. I buried the vessels underground for a month. Then I drank the water. If I was to be made well, the sadhu said the gods would use the water to remove my leprosy. I followed these instructions for one year."

Harry said, "You misunderstand me. I am praying for your soul, Gokul."

The Indian man did not respond.

"You see, Gokul, I cannot promise you my God will heal your body, but I can promise you that He will live inside you if you surrender your life to Him."

"Why would your god want to live inside a leper?"

"The Bible says that God looks on the inside; man looks on the outside. The God I serve loves you just as much as he loves me because He created each of us."

Gokul, who always appeared to be on the verge of stumbling, suddenly diverted from Harry's side, shaking his head, with each step distancing himself from the missionary. The prospect of a God who loved him was more than he could comprehend from one brief conversation. He had to be alone to ponder this revelation.

Harry had yet to master the mindset of Hinduism, so he cherished the presence of Saul—a Hindu convert employed to oversee the lepers. Saul was a hard-working Indian who willingly devoted his life to caring for the needy. Harry dispatched Saul in many instances to talk with Hindus wanting to discuss spiritual matters.

One day Saul came running with news that Gokul had made a decision for Christ. Harry raised both his hands to signify victory, then reached out to shake Saul's hand.

"God has used you, my dear friend," Harry said.

Embarrassed by his employer's praise, Saul merely bowed his head.

"Well done, Saul," he affirmed with the clapping of his hands.

"Thank you, Sahib. I only want to please God."

"That you have done. Your crown in heaven will have many jewels because you have been so faithful."

"Sahib, just as long as my Savior is there and you are there, I will be happy."

Harry was humbled by his worker's comment. It disturbed him to think that any man or woman would idolize him—a man with his frailties—when almighty God was so deserving of praise.

That evening, resting on his pillow, Harry prayed silently, "God, I can do nothing without You. Someday, it will be necessary for another man to carry on this work. I will pass on, but Your work will continue. Keep me humble in Your eyes, and help the workers and lepers to understand that I am merely an instrument. You are the Master who has compassion on them."

Harry's eyelids closed. Meanwhile, the wind whistled outside his bungalow as if the heavens were applauding a man who had a heart after God.

14
Protected by God

Five-year-old Yohan hid behind his uncle, clutching onto the back of the man's leg. Fear registered in his eyes like a boy watching his parents' execution. Disease had ravaged Yohan's family until now only he remained, and for that reason the waif scanned the mission compound with trembling.

"His family is dead and the boy is sick," the uncle explained. "Can you take him? If he stays with us, he will surely die."

Harry was not sure where Yohan could stay, but anywhere was more suitable than the fatal alternative. "Yes, we will take him," the missionary promised.

The boy suffered from a rectal disorder that required some treatment, but within days he was climbing trees and racing across the compound like a rambunctious monkey. From their veranda Harry and Helen laughed at Yohan's youthful exuberance.

"He's got his share of energy," Helen noted.

"He's very special," Harry added. "God has sent him to us for a reason."

Helen peered at her husband, expecting him to elaborate. Instead, he simply repeated, "Yes . . . a special child."

Once the laborers completed the orphanage facility, fifty children ranging in ages from two to sixteen quickly filled the home. Yohan, who lived in the orphanage, became a favorite of the workers. His straight hair was always combed so neatly to one side, and his smooth skin was unblemished. He often played marbles and hopscotch with the Waggoner children, ate at their dinner table, and wore their hand-me-downs.

Bernice also took a liking to Yohan and was in a frenzy when Harry received notification that the boy's relatives were seeking to have him returned to them. They needed him, so they claimed, to work in the fields.

Yohan, sporting his standard attire of cut-offs and a T-shirt, was flying a homemade kite of paper and bamboo when Harry sought out the youngster.

"Hello! That's some kite you have there."

"It's a good day for flying," Yohan responded.

"Yohan, the court has asked for a hearing to see if you should return to your uncle. Do you want to return?"

"Sahib, this is my home. You are my family; the orphans are my brothers and sisters," the boy answered, unruffled by the court's notion.

"Are you sure? Because we will do what we have to for you to stay—if you are sure that is what you want."

Harry stared into the young boy's eyes, each measuring the other's affection.

"Yes, I am sure."

The court judge listened as both sides staked their claim to Yohan's future. By his expressions—a raised eyebrow, a frown, a nod—it appeared as though the judge was siding with the boy's uncle. The Arya Samaj, a radical sect, had also become involved in the case, seizing the opportunity to denounce Christianity and attack American missionaries.

Bernice and Helen prayed and cried as if their own son was being taken from them.

"I do not want to leave you," Yohan said, grabbing Helen's hand.

"God will not allow you to be taken away. Do not worry," she answered.

But secretly, she knew there was a chance the court could rule against them.

Once all the testimonies had been heard, members of the two parties—including Yohan—sat up from the backs of their chairs anticipating the verdict. Hearts were beating and palms perspiring.

The judge asserted, "The Waggoners have invested in this boy, and he wishes to remain with them. The court finds no reason to disrupt this relationship."

Yohan leaped from his chair and skipped to Helen with his arms outstretched, saying, "I love you."

Patting his shiny head, Bernice and Helen said simultaneously, "We love you, too."

Standing close, like a proud father, Harry had to restrain the flow of tears. God had answered his prayers and protected one of his many "adopted" children. Yes, Harry thought, Yohan is special.

Harry returned to court several months later. Another Hindu businessman was vying to void the transfer of property to Harry. Wanting the buildings torn down and the leper homes vacated, he was not about to rest until every Christian was banished. His attorney cited an obscure law that could require Harry to return the property to its former owners and be restored to its previous condition. Naturally, Harry was growing weary of these attacks.

Again, Kanhaiyah Pare came to Harry's defense.

"This man has come to help the leper not for personal gain, nor to receive commendation," Pare told the judge. "He has come because he cares for sick people. He has paid a fair price for the property and filed the necessary papers. If he loses his land, all the land purchases for the past twenty years must be voided."

Pare was a stiff man who wore a white hat and curled his mustache with his fingers. Occasionally he leaned over to Harry and whispered for him not to worry. "You have a signed agreement. It will not be overturned."

The day of the final hearing, Harry set out on foot for the fifteen mile journey to the court building in Bansi. He crossed a temporary bridge—most were temporary because they were washed out by the monsoon floods—then he ambled down a dirt road guarded by slumping trees. It was unusual for a white man to make such a journey on foot, but Harry needed time to pray. He knew everything weighed in the balance of the judge's decision.

The magistrate read his verdict like a housewife reading a shopping list. "Since the land is being used as was stated on the application filed with the court three years ago and the owners agreed to the sale of the property, I hereby declare that the property remain in the hands of its current occupants."

The Hindu businessman who brought the case against Harry rushed from the courtroom, his coat tails flapping.

Harry later heard the man's 4,000-rupee elephant had fallen over dead—the price he paid for attacking God and His anointed.

September was a month for repairing what the monsoon destroyed. It was also a month of contrast, for the winds and rains ceased and the stillness and dryness set in. It was under these conditions that Helen gave birth to Mildred in Uska Bazar while under the care of an Indian physician.

When babies were born in the mission, widows were readily available to serve as midwives. Harry cherished the chance to dedicate these children. Taking them in his arms, he said a prayer of blessing. Tears of joy often cascaded down his cheeks. But nothing brought the satisfaction of dedicating his own children. In fact, Harry and Helen made a habit of rededicating their children to God every night before they fell asleep.

Harry also found pleasure in leading lepers into water baptism. Perhaps none was as fulfilling as the day he finally submerged Nehru—one who had routinely dismissed Harry's teachings as nonsensical. Even so, Nehru attended church regularly. His leprous wife did all she could to dissuade him from entering the chapel, but Nehru insisted it was purely for entertainment. His beliefs would not be poisoned by the white man. For Nehru and his wife, quarreling had become a ritual, their arguments spiriting into the night. She was even more set in her Hindu ways than was Nehru.

Harry had all but given up on converting the couple when one day Nehru and his wife stepped into the line of baptism candidates. Harry's eyes bulged.

"Does this mean you have accepted Christ as your personal Savior?" Harry asked.

"Sahib, that is why I am here. Me and my wife want to change our ways. We want to follow Christ."

Harry was so overjoyed that he buried his face in his wet hands.

Nehru, initially, was puzzled by Harry's reaction.

"Yes, Nehru, I will baptize you. I am just so happy that you have chosen a new life." Then, lowering his friend into the water, Harry recited, "I baptize you in the name of the Father, Son, and Holy Ghost."

Harry waded out of the water that day feeling the swell of relief and accomplishment that Moses must have experienced after crossing the Red Sea.

Later that afternoon, when the missionary felt like throwing a celebration party, all the laughter died in sorrow. The mission entered a state of mourning, for one of the residents slipped into eternity. A soft-spoken woman, Burhia was one of the oldest and most loved lepers. She would be missed.

Because there were no embalmers, the body was immediately washed, wrapped in clothing, and loaded onto a crude bamboo ladder. The ladder was then attached to an oxcart and taken to the burial site. Trailing closely behind the oxcart, in tribute to Burhia, the lepers paraded down the steamy country road to the cemetery two miles away.

As the mummy was dropped into the grave, Harry's voice squealed. "Thank you, Lord, for allowing us to be a part of Burhia's life . . . . We look forward to the day we see her again . . . in heaven." He wanted to say so much more, but the day had been filled with far too much emotion for Harry.

Exhaustion had set in. So, with a breathy tone, he said, "Amen."

As was their tradition, the hired workers played marbles under the same tree day after day. The men huddled around the circle etched in red dirt, yelling like a band of men gambling in a metropolitan alley. The noise was disruptive at first, but soon the missionaries learned to disregard the chaotic sounds. During one of these games Beatrice strayed in the path of a team of oxen. Sensing their awesome presence, Beatrice instinctively yelled and threw up her arms to protect her face. One of the men playing marbles heard the shrill of her voice over the cheers. He shouted to the oxen, "Halt!" As if colliding with a barrier, the team stopped and Beatrice escaped, frightened but unharmed.

Danger seemed to go with the territory. Harry, for example, was reading a much cherished letter from A. G. Ward when he heard Helen yelp mysteriously. He found her in another life-threatening predicament; she had stepped on a karait snake in her bedroom—a harmless-looking monster that is twice as poisonous as a cobra.

The snake was motionless, obviously sizing up its foe, when Harry hammered it with a board.

Willard, peeking over his father's shoulder, said, "You coulda been killed, ya know it, Mom?"

"You could have been killed," she corrected.

"Right," he acknowledged.

The Waggoners had much for which to be thankful. In danger, God had protected them time and again. Despite run-ins with scorpions, snakes, and other venomous creatures, they had survived unscathed.

15
Family Times

Thanksgiving marked a time to celebrate God's provision and Harry and Helen's wedding anniversary. The missionaries and their guests feasted on wild peacock. The natives and the Waggoner children also enjoyed a variety of games and races. The picnic atmosphere was highlighted by exchanging gifts and awarding prizes such as perfumed soap cakes, silk scarves, and Indian candy. Croquet was also a favorite pastime. As the fierce matches wore into the twilight, Harry pointed the Ford's headlights onto the field.

Thanksgiving was one of those rare occasions when the lepers did not cook for themselves. Lepers normally received an allotment of food and water for their respective homes, and they prepared their own meals. Most of the lepers also grew fruit and vegetables in a sizable plot adjoining their home. They took great pride in their gardens, and appeared noticeably pleased when one of the missionaries paid special attention to their work. They valued their fruit and vegetables like nuggets from a treasure chest. In essence, the savory edibles were their statues, their paintings, their masterpieces. Harry understood the depth of their sacrifice when one Sunday they toted baskets of fruit and vegetables to the front of the chapel and laid them beneath the wooden cross.

The lepers were also responsible for washing their own clothes in a rustic tub and then laying them on rocks so they would dry under the scorching sun. It was in those same type of tubs that the children were bathed, and on holidays such as Thanksgiving, that they bobbed for fruit.

Christmas was another festive time—a break from the burden of long work days and responsibility. Lepers received handmade clothing, baskets of food, candy, soap, and for those who could read, literature.

The cooks prepared food for the orphans and lepers, often working all evening to carve out a feast that surpassed that of the previous year. While they worked, they laughed and sang hymns like nightingales on the New England coast.

Before the sun could make a grand entry on Christmas morning, the orphans began chattering at annoying decibels in hopes of chasing away the moon and stars. Before Harry could crawl out of bed, the orphans were mimicking a cathedral choir, neatly stacked in rows and singing "Gloria in Excelsis Deo" with surprising precision. The entire camp and countryside awoke to the sound of their music, led by Saul's beautiful tenor voice, which swept through the air like notes from a chorus of angels.

Without fail, Harry appeared on the veranda to applaud "his children." Soon villagers arrived to listen, too. They were unaccustomed to Western songs, yet, for the most part, they found the music pleasurable.

The Waggoner children knew not to expect much for Christmas; from their earliest memories their father taught them that Christmas was a season to give and a time to reflect on the gift of God's Son. He taught, "This is not the time to think about what you can get for yourself but rather what you can give to another." Each of the children had at least one gift to open. Usually they unwrapped a whittled animal, a homemade necklace, a stitched doll, or a piece of handsewn clothing. Harry and Helen could never bring themselves to spend money that would detract from the work of the colony.

Throughout the year, the Waggoners read the Bible as a family. Camped at the breakfast table, Harry read a chapter every morning to his youngsters. Sometimes following the Bible reading, Harry gave in to the children's wishes and told them a missionary story or one of his hunting tales.

"Okay," he said with an infectious laugh, "I remember some years ago when . . . ." That's how he started every story, but every episode ended with a spiritual lesson. Harry and Helen made it clear each child had to seek his own relationship with God, that their parents would not flank them when they stood before God on Judgment Day.

Some evenings when the children fell asleep on the veranda, under the mosquito nets, they dreamed of that day when they would meet their Creator face to face. The dreams, however, were not nearly as frightening as waking to the sight of a straggling native peering through their nets or a wayward animal rampaging onto the grounds.

One evening the children had already closed their eyes and were moments from entering a deep sleep. A laborer pulled a rope that maneuvered a butterfly-like fan above them. Their father's nightly rendition on the chapel's foot-pump organ began to grow faint. Suddenly, Beatrice let out an alarming scream that awakened the residents of the mission. A man had staggered onto the veranda and was gazing down at them with fierce eyes.

The organ playing stopped. So did the fan.

Troops came running to her aid as the man fled the stampede. Harry cradled his daughter in his arms and brushed his hand through her hair, saying, "It's all right. He's gone. He won't be back."

This same compassionate man was not reluctant to use a razor strap on the children if they were disobedient. Donald certainly led the pack when it came to whippings. Once he threw a mango at his sister from a treetop. Harry bounced the youngster over to the house and bent the sprouting nine-year-old over his knee.

"I love you, son, but you can't go around hitting your sisters."

The child, his deep-set eyes protruding, said, "But I didn't hit anyone."

"That's not the point, Donald. You could have. I told you once before not to throw things at your sisters. You disobeyed me."

Donald cried, but he noted to himself that the whippings at the hand of his father no longer hurt as much. Donald was not sure if his father was losing strength or if his threshold of pain was reaching new heights.

Helen relinquished the disciplining duties to her husband, seldom raising her voice above a monotone pitch. And rarely did she argue with Harry, though on one occasion the couple's voices crescendoed so even the children heard their conversation.

"I don't tell you how to preach, so don't tell me how to cut costs. Don't you think I'm trying?" she asked.

"I'm not saying you're not," Harry retorted. "We just can't have new clothes made for the children every year they go away to school."

"You know as well as I do that they deserve to have something new. They're sacrificing enough already."

"Listen, Helen, I'm not saying they don't, but we have bills to pay. Every little bit saved counts."

"Sometimes, Harry Waggoner, you're as stubborn as a buffalo," Helen said, departing the house into the grizzly sounds of the night: passing trains, animals, distant voices, the rustling of leaves.

Beatrice, keen to the disagreement, wandered after her mother into the chapel. There, face down on a pew, Helen sobbed uncontrollably.

"What's wrong, Mommy?" Beatrice asked.

Helen, though startled by the sound of a familiar voice, kept her head buried in her arms. "Nothing important, honey. Please go back to bed."

Beatrice passed her father as she returned to the house. He was coming to retrieve his beloved spouse.

"Helen," Harry said, lifting her from the pew, "I'm sorry."

She was slow to respond, partly embarrassed by her tirade of tears.

"Helen, I love you."

She bit her lip and sighed.

Harry hugged her head to his chest, then repeated, "I'm in love with you. I'm sorry."

"I love you, too," she whimpered.

"I'm just a little tired."

Helen said, "I know you are." To herself, she affirmed her worst fears: Harry was indeed quietly losing his strength, and she did not know what to do.

Willard, with Donald in his tracks, loved to pepper monkeys with slingshots. Whenever the two lads spotted a huge Langur monkey in an apricot tree, they readied their weapons. Once, just before the sun took its final bow, the boys encountered a feisty gray-furred animal with a black face. The monkey displayed his pointed teeth, trying to ward off his youthful attackers. Undaunted, the boys kept firing at the animal despite its vicious growlings.

Suddenly, the six-foot animal flew from its branch onto the ground like a creature from *The Wizard of Oz*. Willard led the retreat. Donald, sprinting frantically, tripped over a root and sprawled onto the ground. The boy felt his pursuer stalking him, certain the animal would claw him to death. Instead, the monkey slowed down, sneered at the boy, and then vaulted up a tree.

Donald gulped. Willard laughed. The monkey seethed.

"You should have seen your face!" Willard teased. "You are shaking; you were scared."

"It's not funny," Donald snapped. "I could have been killed."

By the time they returned to the mission, Willard and Donald were cackling about their harrowing episode, ready to tell anyone who would listen about their run-in with a "ten-foot" monkey.

The family learned to be cautious around wild animals, especially snakes. Harry was not fond of snakes, even those presumably trained by the natives. He had witnessed the death of a man bitten by a cobra and since then viewed the slithering beasts as nothing more than Satan's pawns. He could still visualize the scene of villagers crowding around the doomed man, scoffing at him, telling him to call on the gods for forgiveness for stepping on one of their snakes, which are considered gods. They threw mustard seeds at the man, believing this would draw the poison from his body. Then they put a brown paste into his ears and nostrils. All the while the man pleaded for mercy, for medical attention. Harry knew if he intervened his life and ministry to these people would be in danger, so from a distance he watched this man pass into eternity. For nights afterwards, Harry dealt with the guilt of that episode.

Some years later, Donald had his own duel with a cobra. He had accompanied Saul on foot to a nearby village to pick up supplies; upon returning home after dark, they noticed under the dim light of the moon that something resembling a huge branch obstructed the road. Donald nearly stepped over the branch when it suddenly came to life—all five feet of it. The cobra raised its head, its gills fanning, its tongue wagging lustfully. Suddenly it struck at

Donald's leg, but he was able to leap out of its path. It prepared for another attack, but Donald clobbered it with an umbrella he was carrying. The snake never knew what hit it as Donald pummeled its head until it showed no signs of life.

The boy ran all the way back to the mission, Saul panting heavily as he tried to keep pace. Helen opened the door.

"What happened? You're as white as a ghost."

Donald was breathless.

Saul spoke up. "Your son has courage. He killed a cobra with my umbrella."

Instantly, Helen turned pale as well, sat down, and said, "Didn't I tell you to stay away from snakes?"

"I did," he said, "but the snake came after me."

Helen looked to Saul to corroborate her son's story.

"Yes, he was very strong," Saul said, shaking his head.

She glanced back at Donald and said, "Be careful. We don't want to have to keep worrying about you and snakes. Do you hear me?"

"Yes. Mom."

Helen rubbed her son's shoulder affectionately. "We love you," she said. "We don't want to lose you."

Donald blushed with the warmth of knowing his parents really did love him.

Their love carried Donald through the lonely months that loomed ahead for the sprouting teenager.

16
Perseverance

Regardless of Helen's warnings, Harry stayed in the plains during the blistering hot season. Helen, meanwhile, accompanied the children to the mountains to enroll them in another year of school.

Helen and the children, unbeknownst to Harry—the man who seemed so strong and sure of his decision to stay behind—cried when his family boarded the train in Uska Bazar. Helen would be back in eight weeks, but he would not see his children for nine months.

Not even his pith helmet could shield him from the sun's blast. As he worked in the fields and tended to the lepers, Harry sometimes wondered if his helmet was melting in the 100-plus temperatures. The long hours in the sun baked his skin brown; he began looking like one of the natives. Although the sun had gone into remission at night, the humidity was still suffocating. Sleeping two hours at a time quickly took its toll on Harry's body, and exhaustion soon incapacitated him. He laid in his bed for two days unable to treat the hurting, unable to feed the hungry.

Leaving the children to return to the mission was difficult for Helen. She was tempted to stay, but she knew Harry needed help in preparing for the Northern India

Missionary Convention, which was to be held in Uska Bazar. When Helen arrived home, she found Harry back on his feet but looking more sickly than ever.

"Didn't I tell you this would happen? Look at you!" Helen scolded, pulling him by the arm to his bed. "You're going to stay here until you're well."

"I can't. We have to get ready for the convention."

"We can take care of that. Just stay where you are. And one more thing."

"What?"

"I missed you," Helen said with a kiss on his cheek.

The convention was a highlight for the missionaries. Having an opportunity to exchange praise reports and share needs was therapeutic, but, moreover, it was an opportunity to seek God corporately.

From the borders of Afghanistan, from the snowy heights of Darjeeling, from south of Poona, from the borders of Bengal and the United Provinces, missionaries came for the week-long conference. Harry mustered the strength to speak in the evening services to nearly one hundred missionaries. Never having seen so many Western-ers gathered under one tent, the natives thought they were being invaded.

The missionaries prayed well into the night, anointing and laying hands on each other, asking God to supply their needs and give them protection.

When the week of meetings came to a close, and oxcarts were loaded and trains disembarked with missionaries aboard, Harry and his team felt like orphans—like children returning from a summer camp. They would not see many of their comrades until next year's event. Others they would never see again, for they would not survive on the mission field for twelve more months. That thought alone left Helen in a melancholy mood. But within hours, the energetic faces of her children lifted her spirits and she was herself again.

Shortly after the convention, Harry led a young man of twenty-five to Christ. Bihan had lived in the leper home for nearly two years before notifying Harry he was ready to accept the Christian faith. Harry had no reservations concerning the leper's sincerity when the new believer asked to be baptized. Thus, he was one of seven lepers who wended their way through plowed fields to the river one morning.

Harry placed his hand on Bihan's back and dipped the convert into the water and out again with a splash. Like a well-cued radio commercial, the lepers standing on the bank burst into singing with their raspy voices. Though the music was less than melodious, to Harry it was like a well-rehearsed choir.

Tears welled up in Bihan's eyes as he ran from the water yelling, "Jesus has saved me! Jesus loves me."

Harry waved the next parishioner into the water, trying to rinse the tears from his own face. A young lad walked slowly into the passive current, grimacing because of the chilly water.

"Willard, do you love Jesus?" he asked his son.

The young boy nodded his head. "Yes."

"Have you surrendered your life to Jesus?"

"Yes."

"Then I baptize you in the name of the Father, the Son and the Holy Ghost, amen."

Willard emerged from the river, snorting water from his mouth and nose.

Then Donald, Beatrice, and Almeta took their turns entering the water for baptism. Helen beamed incessantly from the shore. Harry, on the other hand, let tears rinse his face, for it was his way of expressing his gratitude to God for faithfully caring for his children.

When lepers were converted, it always astounded Harry how, without coercing, they shared their faith in God. They seized every opportunity to witness to an unbeliever. It was common to see a trio of lepers walking toward the village Katka or Uska Bazar just to tell heathens about Jesus. Their haggard bodies limped down the smoky trail like children plodding their way to kindergarten. Along the way they initiated conversations with travelers about the love of Jesus.

Invariably, someone asked, "If this Jesus loves you, why are you lepers?"

"Jesus has given us eternal life," they replied. "We are only here for a short time, but in heaven He will reward us with new bodies. Your heathen gods take blood; Jesus gave His blood so we could live."

Occasionally, they led a stranger back to the mission where Harry or one of the other missionaries could answer questions and lead them in the sinner's prayer.

Raghunath, in particular, was uninhibited when it came to preaching the gospel to newcomers. Outside the gate, sitting in his wagon—his version of a soap box—he would quote from the Bible and Harry's sermons.

One day, while Saul was pulling the evangelist-leper in a wagon, his ears perked to the faint voice of a man who waved them closer.

Saul stooped to speak to the beggar lying in a fence of bushes. "What are you in need of?" Saul asked.

"Friend," the man squeaked, "my legs are paralyzed, and I have no one to help me. My village will not permit me to stay in my house. I was told that the Burra Sahib (big gentleman) loved all poor people, so they loaded me on an oxcart and dropped me here during the night."

"My dear man," Saul answered, "this is a home for lepers. As it is, we are overcrowded."

"Please, talk to the Sahib."

Saul stared at the man and then wandered through the gate, listening as Raghunath shouted across the way, "Do you know Jesus? He loves you. Do you have Him in your heart?"

Saul was too far away to hear the man's response.

Moments later, Saul dashed out the entryway to the man's side. "You are fortunate, my friend. The Sahib has ordered that a small hut be constructed just for you."

The eyes of the man swelled, as though he had been unduly praised and rewarded.

"Why does he do this for the leper, for the poor?" the man asked. "I cannot repay him."

Saul answered with a smile. "He does this because his God has told him to help you."

The invalid, in his mid-fifties, shook his head. "Who is this God who has told him to help me?"

"I will tell you more," Saul said, "but first the Sahib asked that you be fed and bathed."

Again the man's face was overwhelmed, like a prince walking into his palace for the first time.

For three days, Saul neglected some of his duties so he could spend time with the curious man. Edith had informed Saul the man was dying, so Saul felt an urgency to lead him to Christ.

Even though the man had not openly confessed Christ as his Savior, he asked Saul if he could be baptized. Saul conferred with Harry who advised the man be given more time to digest the meaning of baptism and salvation. But the man insisted, saying, "You have not told me so, but I know I am dying. Before I go, I want to be one of you. Please, lead me to Jesus."

That afternoon, with the help of Saul and several workers, the invalid was carried into the river where Harry baptized him.

Five days later he died in his sleep, peacefully.

Many lepers experienced slow, agonizing deaths. At times they pleaded for the workers to put them out of their misery. Although Harry loved the lepers, he detested the sight of their rotting bodies. He could almost feel the pain of those with severe cases, yet he could not bring himself to let them die.

Some of the missionary's saddest moments, however, involved the deaths of those who had rejected Jesus Christ. Harry knew he would not see them again. During his moments of quietude, he fought feelings of failure and guilt—as though he were to blame for their decision to deny Christ. But then a glimmer of truth calmed the assault, and he recognized he had truly done all he could.

17
The Beating

The long-sleeved cotton dresses worn by the Waggoner girls certainly helped retain heat and perspiration during the hot, humid season. Their cumbersome pith helmets yielded further discomfort. Despite feeling helplessly miserable, they knew there was little to be gained by complaining, particularly in the presence of their father.

"Beatrice," Harry chided his daughter when she grumbled, "you better move to the North Pole where it's cold."

When the season's first rain clouds converged overhead, the Waggoner children were among the most grateful. For much of the hot season, though, the children were at school in the mountains where it was cooler. And there, rather than toiling in bulky clothes and helmets, students were required to wear straw hats and a standard uniform: black socks, navy blue shorts and white shirts for the boys; black stockings, navy blue skirts and white blouses for the girls.

Worse than the heat was the arduous three-day trip on three different trains to school. It was a tiresome ordeal for the children: seven hundred miles of farmland, wild animals, and villages. There were two bunks in their compartment to share, except for the last leg of the journey on the "toy train." It was a smaller locomotive that traveled from the plains of Siliguri to the heights of Darjeeling. It did not have toilets, so during one trip, they had to hang outside the window to relieve themselves. The compartments were less than comfortable, yet it was the separation from their parents that made this trip so unbearable.

Because there were no phones on campus and even a telegram took several days, only Helen's letters helped ease the pangs of loneliness for the children. Playing soccer, competing in tennis, and climbing Tiger Hill—from where they could observe Mount Everest—helped to pass the time. Regardless of the games and mild climate, each of the Waggoner children would have preferred living in the sun-drenched mission. They missed being with their parents, playing with the orphans, and helping the lepers.

The student body in the private school was comprised of the children of missionaries and wealthy British businessmen. Regardless, teachers did not hesitate to slap the wrists of children who misbehaved. Some ruffians were sentenced to sitting outside their bungalow for entire afternoons. Others were forced to sacrifice snacks and recesses.

Sometimes punishment went too far. Beatrice, for example, wet her bed. For such a crime it was customary to require the child to drape the wet sheet over her head while her classmates marched around her tauntingly.

"Please don't tell the dorm mother," Beatrice pleaded with the nursemaid. "I won't do it again. I promise."

"I'm sorry," the nursemaid responded, "I have to obey the rules."

Beatrice grimaced with tears, causing the nursemaid to retrace her steps toward the young girl.

The young woman hovered over Beatrice for an instant, then said, "Don't cry. I won't say anything. Just this once, but if you ever do it again . . . ."

Lifting her head, Beatrice tried to say "thank you," but her chin was shivering too much to eke out a single word.

Don also had an unfortunate disciplinary experience. He and a friend were discovered carving their initials into an old, discarded desk. The headmaster, Mr. Wright, an American in his mid-thirties, ordered ten-year-old Donald into his office.

"Why were you destroying school property?"

"It was old; it was being thrown away."

"Did it belong to you?"

"No."

"Then what right did you have to carve it up?"

"I don't know; I didn't think it would matter."

"It does matter!" he yelled, sliding the lock on the door.

"Why, if it wasn't going to be used?"

"Young man, lower your pants."

Stunned by the order, Donald searched the headmaster's red face. The boy thought it peculiar that such a "sin" would require a whipping, but he figured it would result in no more than six lashes. But the sixth swat came and went and the headmaster's arm was still administering the walking stick. Within moments, he received twenty lashes. The boy twisted his head to plead with his executioner, as if to ask, "Isn't that enough?" His back was already numb.

Suddenly, the metal cap on the end of the stick flew off, lacerating Donald's arm. Still, the headmaster continued his assault.

Finally, the torture stopped.

Donald could not rise to his feet, weaving in and out of consciousness.

"Get up!" the headmaster demanded. "If you ever damage school property again, you'll receive another whipping. Do you hear me?"

The boy was not coherent enough to respond. Somehow he crawled to his bed.

The following morning, Willard stood at the end of his brother's mattress. "Let's get going. It's time to get up," he called.

Donald remained motionless.

"Get up, Don!" he shouted, rolling his brother over to wake him. His hand brushed against something slimy and raw, thinking at first the youngster had been sweating. Looking at his hand with great alarm, Willard found it red with blood.

"Don, you're bleeding!" He pushed his brother onto his side and lifted his shirt. The scrambled skin scared Willard at first, but soon his emotions turned to anger.

"Who did this?"

"Mr. Wright," Donald slurred.

"He's going to pay for this," Willard growled.

The young man had no perception of the severity of his condition. He had gone to bed just knowing the pain was more horrible than he had ever encountered, feeling like an elk must when wounded by a hunter's arrow.

Harry received a telegram from Willard a few days after the incident, informing him that Donald had been taken to a doctor. Willard wrote, "Dad, the doctor said he has more than fifty stripes on his back from the whipping."

Rage surfaced in Harry to an unfamiliar degree. He dispatched word to a missionary near the school to check on his son, though wishing he were there to handle Mr. Wright himself. The leper home was facing some serious difficulties, so Harry had to disdain any such notion. He hid the telegram from Helen, knowing there was no need to get her upset until he garnered all the facts.

Harry's missionary friend visited Donald and confirmed the near slaying. He set Harry's mind at ease, nonetheless, saying, "Donald will be okay; he is out of danger, but this man should be taken to court."

Harry sat at a table reading his Bible one afternoon, pondering some form of action against the teacher. He weighed whether a lawsuit would send a conflicting message to the natives. He asked himself, "Would it be viewed as a contradiction to my teaching of love and forgiveness?"

Then, unexpectedly, Willard appeared outside Harry's bungalow.

Harry dashed into the open air to be reunited with his firstborn. A few strides from his son, the missionary's smile turned to a look of consternation.

"What are you doing away from school?"

The handsome young man looked away from his father while saying, "They expelled me."

"Expelled! What for?"

"For threatening to get even with Mr. Wright for hurting Don."

Harry started to scold his son but was interrupted.

"Dad," Willard said on the verge of tears, "you should have seen his back. And when I heard you couldn't come, I just wanted to do something to make Mr. Wright pay."

Harry softly cradled the boy's head in his arms and asked, "What did you do to him, son?"

"Nothin'. Someone told him I was gonna . . . and he expelled me. I'm sorry, Dad. I just had to pay him back."

Harry started to give Willard a sermonette on the evils of revenge, but he kept the Scriptures to himself. His own hostilities were such that his words would have been hypocritical. If the chance ever availed itself, Harry was inclined to land a few jabs of his own to Mr. Wright's jaw.

18
Hunting Trophies

Harry's younger brother, George, the twelfth of fourteen children, was waiting for his nieces and nephews when they returned from school on the railtrain one day in November 1926. George was not as angular as Harry, but he had a similar affection for laughter. Routinely, he showed off the distinguishable gap between his two front teeth when he smiled. George was also a musician. He and his brother often played their instruments well into the night, that is until George's fiance, Katie, took up residence in the mission.

Katie was an attractive, modest girl who came to India just prior to their wedding. The natives surrounded the entrance of the mission with garlands of flowers, celebrating her arrival. As she rode into the compound, natives lined each side of the lane as if saluting a brigadier general. They smiled and chanted for her, the affectionate welcome inviting a well-deserved grin to the young woman's ivory-smooth face.

George unloaded her bags as, one by one, the native workers, missionaries, and Waggoner children stepped forward to extend their greetings. An unusually festive mood filled the camp, as everyone—missionaries and lepers alike—anticipated the wedding ceremony.

Katie brought with her a beautiful wedding dress. So gorgeous was the material and design that even the natives marveled as she walked the center aisle of the chapel.

George was beaming more than ever, his hair slicked down with a special ointment given to him by one of the workers. His suit was wrinkled, but the flower attached to his lapel and his neat tie compensated for the imperfections.

The two lovers moved into the bungalow where Bernice and the other missionaries once stayed. With a wife to care for, and living two miles away, George wisely refrained from staying up half the night serenading the fields with his trombone.

But not even marriage could calm Uncle George's flare for adventure.

One afternoon, with the sun at its pinnacle, a native raced frantically to George's side, claiming to have seen a man-eating alligator.

"Grab your rifle, Harry, and let's go see," George said.

George enjoyed throwing his homemade fishing poles into the river. He and Saul chaperoned the nieces and nephews on fishing excursions whenever their workload was light. So George never wanted to miss an opportunity to kill the monstrous pests who jeopardized his recreational fun at the river.

Sneaking through the grass, Harry and his squadron of natives spotted the alligator sunning on a sandbar.

"Shhh!" Harry sounded.

He raised his 30-30 Savage rifle. Donald put his fingers in his ears. The shot hit the beast just below the eye, causing it to tumble into the water and sink to the bottom.

The expedition team walked cautiously to the river's edge, only to discover the victim had fallen into a ten-foot hole.

Harry peered at one of the natives. "Go down and wrap a rope around it, and we'll pull it out."

"No, Sahib, not me." The native stepped backward and waved his hands.

George spoke up. "I'll do it."

Harry shook his head as if to say, "Are you crazy?"

But before he could convince his brother otherwise, George had stripped to his shorts and was in the water.

Moments later, everyone, including the children, were pulling on the rope. Once the dead creature was on shore, some of the natives took turns riding its tail. It took ten men to load the beast onto an oxcart.

Back at the compound, the natives swarmed around the oxcart to get a look at Harry's eighteen-foot trophy. The Waggoner boys acted like medical students observing a delicate operation as the natives removed the hide. One of the natives handed Donald an egg extracted from the animal's stomach. It was as tough as the exterior of a soccer ball. Donald proceeded to throw it into the air and catch it again.

"Put that down!" Helen ordered. "It's dirty."

Donald obliged.

Meanwhile, Harry was busy fielding congratulatory words from the natives for his marksmanship.

Hunting for nilgai antelope brought far more fulfillment to Harry than shooting alligators. They were blue-gray galled animals, larger than mule deer and smaller than elk. There was no hunting season, and the natives were always willing to help if they were guaranteed a portion of the meat. Whenever the food supply dwindled, Harry and George set out on a mini-safari usually as near as five miles from camp. The natives beat drums and used bamboo sticks to scare the nilgai from the bush into a clearing where the two missionaries were waiting to complete the ambush. On occasion, they landed a black buck or wild pig, but a 350-pound nilgai that pillaged farmers' crops and had delicious meat was the prized trophy.

When Harry, George, and their crew returned from one hunting excursion, they stirred the natives in the compound from their haunches. Mouths began to salivate and eyes swelled as an enormous but dead nilgai was paraded down "main street." Because there was no refrigeration, the meat had to be eaten right away. Everyone anticipated receiving a generous portion.

Harry and George—the warriors—marched into camp amidst a medley of cheers from the compound's inhabitants. Choosing not to assume credit, they smiled and politely tipped their pith helmets. "God has provided," they declared. "We will eat well tonight."

It was not a festive occasion for the two sportsmen, though. They had just completed their final hunting expedition together. George had accepted an invitation to coordinate a missionary project near Ranchi, west of Calcutta, and he would be leaving for his new assignment within a few days. The two brothers did not embrace that day, nor utter a sentimental farewell speech. They knew it was the end of an era, but neither wanted to speak his thoughts . . . until they had to.

19
Losing Loved Ones

April 1928, before the monsoon showered its first drop of rain, a water tank was installed with the help of a one-time plumber who had joined the missionary ranks. The American worker put in a windmill that brought water from the well to the 5,000 gallon holding tank; from there it was distributed to the various houses. The windmill became a tourist attraction of sorts. Villagers traveled many miles just to see this peculiar structure. And when a windcharger was added years later, the mission was illuminated with lightbulbs.

With the installation of septic tanks, the camp also gained flushing toilets and wash basins in the buildings. Before the renovation, outhouses had to be routinely emptied in the fields and clean water delivered to the rooms in buckets.

Saul appreciated the modernizations, but he especially enjoyed watching the windmill spin. When Edith confined him to bed, that pleasure was snatched from him. He was coughing up dark saliva and having difficulty keeping his food down.

Edith alerted Harry that Saul's sickness could be life-threatening.

"Saul, my dear friend," Harry said, "I have come to pray for you."

"Thank you, Sahib. You are my friend and a man from God. Yes, please pray," Saul rasped.

Harry placed his hand on the man's stomach and asked for God to restore Saul's body to health. Harry—still lacking strength himself—was full of faith and hope that his co-worker would recover.

During a baptism ceremony one week later, a messenger boy brought word to the missionary that his friend had died during his sleep.

Harry raced from the water—almost as if he thought he could do something to resurrect his "Lazarus."

An hour before Saul's burial, Harry sat at his desk, staring, shaking his head at an empty wall. He wanted to cry, but he couldn't. A myriad of sorrows danced in his mind, but he could muster no emotion. Fatigue had emptied his well of tears. His trance was broken by the sound of the hobbling herd of lepers making their way to the cemetery to bury their beloved Saul, the man who had led many of them to Jesus Christ. Harry picked himself from his chair and entered the procession.

The dismal trek to Saul's gravesite was, for Harry and Helen, one more regret in a volume of defeats and victories. India, the endearing land, had swallowed another loved one. The grief they were experiencing could only be overcome by thoughts of Saul standing by his Savior's side.

It was common for villagers to abandon children at the feet of missionaries. The stories were often heart-wrenching. One day an elderly man brought a dark-skinned girl to the mission. The child, about to be burned alive with one of her dead parents, was rescued by the old man from a heap of burning wood. The child—so the village council determined—was possessed by evil spirits. Because both parents died shortly after her birth, she was pegged the culprit.

This big-eyed child was as gentle as a cuddling kitten, even though her stomach was protruding from malnutrition. Beatrice, having seen her mother play doctor, used soap as a suppository and soon discovered she was discharging worms from the little girl.

Another child was brought into the compound the following day. Piati's husband had threatened to kill the child because he wanted a son. Thus, the frightened mother fled to the colony to escape her husband and turn the child over to the orphanage. In some parts of India, women had few rights; they were virtual slaves to their husbands, so Piati feared she would be forced to surrender the child to her husband should he opt to carry out his threats.

She found asylum with the missionaries.

Bernice was informing Harry and Helen of her housing plans for the two new girls when a messenger on bicycle pedaled through mud puddles into the compound. With him he carried a telegram addressed to Harry. It read: "Father died of physical complications. Funeral already held when you receive this. Sorry you could not be with us."

Helen asked, "What is it?"

Harry's forehead puckered and his eyes twitched.

"What is it?" Helen repeated.

"It's Dad," he whispered. "He . . . ."

Helen knew by her husband's ghastly reaction that God had called John Waggoner home.

There were no planes to transport Harry to the States for the funeral, or enough money or time to take an ocean liner. Harry merely crumbled the telegram into his pocket and retired to his office where he could weep in peace.

20
Battling Poverty and Disease

Gurdin was a mason by trade. He helped Harry supervise and train his workers—a crew of ten skillful men from nearby villages. The Indian—a gift from God, Harry claimed—was a stout man with rough hands and a graying mustache. Hour after hour he and Harry worked together building brick molds. The men loaded clay into the molds and scraped away the excess with a string. To protect the bricks from thieves, Harry's initials were etched on each brick. Then they were transported to the drying mound and from there to the huge man-made kiln for baking.

The crew remodeled the bungalow at Uska Bazar, built additional homes for the lepers, refurbished the school at Hardoi, and built churches and living quarters for various missionaries in the province. Even more significant than the construction taking place was the effect Harry was having on the spiritual lives of Hindus and Muslims serving on his work crew. Some were even bold enough to ask him questions about the Christian God.

Whatever confidence the men held in Harry nearly evaporated when the mission's funds were depleted and payday for the crew was swiftly approaching. Harry feared the men would revolt if they were not paid.

The entire missionary family knelt in the Waggoner home and prayed God would provide the necessary money. They had no sooner prayed a simple prayer when a knock came to the door.

"Brother Waggoner," said a Swedish missionary who lived twenty-five miles away, "how are you?"

Harry was a little baffled by the unexpected visit and stuttered, "Well, hello" before shaking the man's hand.

In unison everyone rose to their feet and the children were signaled to retreat to the other room.

"Won't you please come in?"

"Most assuredly, yes, thank you."

The white-haired missionary fell into a chair and then asked Helen, "Could I ask for some water? That's a long trip on a bicycle for a man my age."

Astounded by the man's journey, Harry asked, "What has brought you all this way?"

"I just felt inclined to pay you a social call." That did not relieve Harry's curiosity, but he let the issue rest. They enjoyed a lengthy visit before the man stood to leave.

"Thank you for coming, Brother Hanson," Harry said.

"I enjoyed our chat very much. Harry, I wanted you to know that God wouldn't let me sleep last night. He told me you were in need and that I was to bring you one hundred rupees. Isn't that right? Isn't that what you need?"

Harry's cheeks became red, his eyelids preparing to entertain tears. "God never fails us. Thank you for listening to God. Yes, that's exactly what we needed by this afternoon to pay our workers. We were just praying for God's help when you arrived."

The two men embraced, and the elder missionary settled onto his bicycle. "Yes, well, just know God heard your request. He is honored by your work, Brother Waggoner."

"Thank you for your encouragement. We all need to hear that from time to time," Harry said.

"That we do, my dear friend."

"Dad," Doris asked one evening while playing with him in his office, "how much money do you get for working here?"

"I don't receive any money; why do you ask?"

"I don't know. I see that the workers get paid, so I was just wondering."

"We get paid in other ways. God provides all we need. And besides, the less money we take the more lepers we can help."

Doris thought about that for a moment then scampered into the other room.

His daughter's inquisition propelled Harry into a moment of introspection. By himself, he recalled all the work A. G. Ward had done to supply funds. He pondered how it cost only thirty-five dollars a year to support a leper, and yet there were so many in need of help. He thought of the future and Willard and Donald, who were quickly approaching adulthood. He also considered *his* future and the need to make the natives self-sufficient, so they would not be dependent on the white man.

This concern prompted Harry to begin vocational training programs where natives learned special skills such as construction, sewing, farming, and making cloth. From the moment the sun burst onto the scene until it made its exit, natives pumped their sewing machines with their feet. Some of the women Helen trained excelled in their craft. Their work would have made fashion designers envious. These native women tailored most of the clothing worn in the mission.

Willard and Donald, however, wanted to hide when the tailors started sizing them for new outfits. The boys felt conspicuous by the special attention given them when orphans were relegated to wearing *their* hand-me-downs.

The women tailors had their first crack at making clothing for a baby when Homer was born in April 1929. He was a healthy, robust youngster—an unexpected but welcomed addition to the Waggoner household.

On several occasions, the family nearly lost one of the other children. Almeta survived a turbulent childhood. Besides a scorpion bite, she also incurred an eye disease known as "aankee" in Hindustani. Her eyes swelled so badly she looked like an alien, her forehead bulging grotesquely. For almost a week the Waggoners confined her to a dark room, away from the piercing brightness of the tropical sun. Neither experience, however, compared to the suffering Doris endured in 1930 at Gorakhpur Hospital, a British-run facility near the boarding school. Since four of their daughters were getting their tonsils removed, Harry and Helen made the lengthy journey to be near their children during the ordeal.

From the outset of the operation, Doris began swallowing blood. The stitches refused to hold.

Perspiration formed into hundreds of globules on the physician's face.

Doris began screaming deliriously, the hemorrhaging increasing. Suddenly her eyes rolled back as though having a seizure.

Harry and a nurse held her to the table while the doctor attempted to stop the bleeding.

Instantly the commotion stopped.

Harry glared at the doctor in an uncharacteristic fashion. "Why are you stopping?"

Tears surfaced in the doctor's eyes. "I've done all I can do. The stitches just won't hold."

Lashing back, Harry ordered, "Try it one more time!"

While the doctor resumed the procedure, Harry and Helen prayed aloud.

"Dear God, save my little girl!" Harry pleaded. "Help these stitches to hold. Please, dear Lord. Help us."

Helen babbled a prayer beneath a drizzle of tears.

The doctor wiped his eyes and said with a tone of surprise, "I think we may have done it. They're holding!"

"Praise God," Harry shouted. "Praise God!"

Helen put her hands to her mouth, covering her blossoming smile.

"Thank You, Jesus," Harry said, "and thank you, doctor."

The doctor's face shined like that of a child, saying, "This was the work of God, sir. I'm the first to admit that."

It was unusual for Bernice to be ill, despite her constant mingling with sickly patients. Thus, when she contracted a fever, Harry and the other missionaries took it seriously. They took turns praying beside her sickbed and reading her Scripture. Harry took the evening shift, thus gravely diminishing his own amount of rest.

Wet rags were placed on her forehead with regularity, and she had to be forced to eat. Still the fever remained. Edith and a visiting doctor were unable to diagnose its source, and moving Bernice to a distant hospital was out of the question—although they feared they might lose her if they did not do something. All they could do was pray.

It took weeks for her to begin showing signs of recovery, but the weakening effects of the illness lingered for months. It was apparent she would have to return to America to make a full recovery.

Without her, Harry was left short-handed at a time when his own health was not exemplary. He had denied himself rest and proper food so others could eat. Somehow he was able to collect the strength to function each day.

Then word came his mother was seriously ill. There, in his bungalow one tropical evening, the wearied missionary fell to his knees, partly because he was exhausted and partly out of concern for his mother. He began to admit to himself the inevitable: he too had to return home for a period of rest.

When Helen entered the room, she was dumbfounded by Harry's posture, and even more so by the scowl on his face.

"What's the matter?" she asked.

"I . . . I . . . just found out that my mother is very sick. They're not sure she's going to make it." Helen dropped the garment in her hands and came to his side—though he was perched on his knees—and pressed his head against her hip.

"Honey, I think we should go home. You need to see your mother and rest."

In the past, Harry rebuffed such suggestions, but this time his arguments waned. "What about . . . ?"

Helen glared at her husband. "We need to go home."

"We can't just leave . . . ."

"Yes we can. Edith can stay with the children at school, and we can take Homer back with us."

Harry tried to find a valid excuse, but Helen stood firm. "We need to go," she said. "You know I'm right."

Harry bowed his head and said, "I guess so . . . ."

21
Back to India

After seventeen months on furlough, Bernice's return to the mission was like that of a war hero. Saluting her with hearty salaams and laughter, the lepers stood in front of their homes like fans hoping to catch a glimpse of a celebrity as she rode into the compound in the back seat of the black Ford. All that was missing was the ticker-tape.

Children from the orphanage barreled down the gravel path, kicking up a tornado of dust. Then they lined up and began singing a song they learned for the grand occasion.

A healthy Bernice wiped tears from her face, then said, "It's wonderful to be home, to be with all of you again. I missed you so much."

Her tears kept dripping like rain from a rooftop.

The natives clapped and cheered.

The aging missionary became embarrassed by the reception, saying, "Now, now, when Sahib Waggoner returns, *he* is the one who is deserving of such applause."

"When will they return?" a hairy-chinned leper asked.

"Soon, very soon. They love you all too much to stay away very long."

The crowd of lepers chattered with excitement, for they would soon be reunited with their "family."

By early 1931, Harry and Helen were fit to return to the mission. It had been a torturous twelve months: dealing with the death of Lulu and the separation from their children and the lepers and orphans they had adopted as their own.

Upon their return, the couple brought with them twenty-seven-year-old missionary Anne Eberhardt. A graduate of Bible college, Anne raised her own financial support so she could serve in India without being a burden to the mission.

As the Waggoners deboarded the train in Uska Bazar, their children came running like greyhounds chasing a locomotive. All of a sudden, Mildred, who had boils on her legs, fell and scraped her knees. The skin was torn away, but the young girl picked herself up and hurried after the others as if nothing had happened. Not even a little pain could distract her eyes from the visage of her loving parents. The family piled onto one another like a team of athletes celebrating a championship season—with Mildred caught in the middle of the stack.

Anne, meanwhile, looked on, a smile monopolizing her rosy cheeks, her curly hair blowing in the wind. A group of Indian men sat admiring her pretty pearl skin as though she were a goddess sent to bring them a moment of beauty. Had she lingered at the depot much longer, they would have fallen to their knees and worshiped her.

Anne was immediately cast into the world she came to serve. One morning a man from a nearby village set a miniature girl in her arms. The child was clothesbare, save a cord around her waist with a Hindu charm attached. Her hair was like a handful of straw, dirt caked around the edges of her eyes.

"Who does this child belong to?" Anne asked the delivery man.

"This child has no one. The mother expired and, as is the custom, they were going to bury the child alive with her. I told them to give her to me instead . . . that the white man would take the child."

Anne and the matron glanced into the forsaken child's foggy eyes and, without asking Harry's permission, said, "Yes, we'll take her."

The man bent at the waist as if to say "thank you," then left the camp never to be seen again.

Anne bathed the child and adorned her in a simple white dress. The one-year-old giggled and smiled as Anne tickled the child's stomach and made funny faces.

She named the girl Praphulit, which means "happiness."

As the youthful missionary looked into the girl's eyes, she realized for the first time why Harry, Helen, Bernice, and others lived beyond a vast ocean, far removed from luxury. They came to offer medical assistance and sustenance, but they also came to offer hope only found in knowing Jesus Christ.

A revelation of the desperate needs around her and the responsibility of raising an infant suddenly befell Anne. For a long while she sat on the veranda, the girl asleep, locked in her arms. Anne studied the compound like a bird protecting her firstborn.

Tears came to her eyes. She tried to wipe them dry without waking Praphulit. "God, why are there so many hurting people—children who need homes and love? Why is there so much tragedy? Why do they have to suffer?"

Anne had dealt with these issues in Bible college, but, for a weak moment, all the biblical answers seemed insufficient.

"Dear God . . . there are so many dying."

Just when Anne's conversation climaxed, Praphulit opened her eyes. She peered at her new mother, smiled, then wet her dress. Anne leaped to her feet after noticing a wet spot on her lap.

Looking toward heaven, Anne could only laugh and marvel at God's sense of humor.

22
A Difficult Decision

In the fall of 1932, the day came that Harry and Helen had avoided discussing. Although they did not want to admit it, their two oldest boys were becoming men and needed to be sent to the States for higher education. Willard was old enough to enter Bible college, and Donald was fifteen.

Willard and Donald both resisted the suggestion. India was their home. Not even the lure of American comforts enticed them. They wanted to remain, to be with their friends and help the lepers. Having spent so many months away at boarding school, the two boys argued for the right to live in the mission . . . at least for a while.

"There's going to be no further discussion on this matter," Harry declared. "Now, I appreciate your desire to stay and help us, but you need to go to college. If God calls you to India, that's fine. Nothing would make me happier."

"But, Dad, why do I need to go to Bible college? I'm helping you already without it," Willard said.

Donald nodded his head in agreement.

"You're leaving. Now is the time and that's final."

The boys knew Harry did not want them to leave; they knew he hoped that God would call them to return one day to continue the work. So it was with a multitude of questions and conflicting thoughts that Willard and Donald prepared to board a train that would take them from their adopted country.

Harry set his hands on their shoulders and said, "I want you both to know that I have only one regret: I wish I would have spent more time with you. I love you boys; you know that. I'm going to miss you."

Helen dried her tears with a handkerchief and stared sadly at her two sons, soaking up each second as if she would never embrace them again. Harry turned his head away from the boys so they would not see his cascading tears.

Little did they know the years that would pass before their next visit. For Donald, it would be fourteen years before he would set eyes on his father.

Donald had every intention of returning to work with his parents, but his father wrote him a letter that altered his course: "Don, I do not want you to come back to India unless God has called you. Don't come just because you're comfortable here. Make sure you're called."

After much inner debate, Donald decided that God had another work for him to do. Willard, meanwhile, throughout Bible school, sought God's will for his life. Alone in his room at night, he often prayed, "I want to go back, but if it's not Your will, Lord, show me."

The missionaries and the native workers, in 1933, endured long, dreadful days, tending to patients by the hour. Cholera swept from village to village like a swarm of locusts attacking a plantation. Harry, Helen, Beatrice, and others knew what to expect: the sleepless nights, the repetitive verses of coughing, the stream of villagers needing care.

The sight of death was uglier than Anne had ever imagined. Sickness gave off a stench she could not avoid.

Furthermore, she was growing homesick; so some nights, when the tension and torment was strong, Anne cried herself to sleep.

Harry and Helen, upon hearing her weeping, told their children to go to her bungalow and give her a "big hug." "Tell her how much you love her and how glad you are that she is here," they instructed.

"Miss Anne," Almeta said with a smile, "I just wanted to say I love you."

Instantly, Anne's tears ceased and she embraced the child.

"Thank you, honey."

That was all she needed to garner the courage for another day.

While Harry, Helen, and Bernice were away one afternoon, Anne was left in charge. As many as ten villagers were dying each day in the greater Uska Bazar area from cholera. Suddenly, like protesters in a labor union squabble, a throng of natives marched toward the compound.

Anne asked fearfully, "What are they doing?"

One of the native pastors answered, "They are asking the goddess of cholera to please leave their village and to come to our compound."

"What should we do?" Anne stuttered as she examined their hateful faces.

"Nothing, Miss Anne; they will not harm us. This is just their way," the pastor shrugged.

Like an undercover spy, Anne sneaked inside her bungalow and into a back room. There she broke into prayer. "Dear Jesus, protect us from this mob . . . and may no disease harm this place."

Anne stayed on her knees until she could sigh with relief, knowing the delegation had disbursed.

"Miss Anne!" hollered one of the pastors. "Miss Anne, they have gone away."

The missionary put her hands to her hair as if molding it into shape and walked outside, thanking God for His deliverance and praying the cholera would not invade the compound.

God answered her prayers. While surrounding villages were stricken and many natives died, the leper home was spared.

It was Bernice who helped Anne sort through her lonely moments and doubts. Anne admired Bernice's perseverance and finally asked her one evening, "Do you ever have times when you want to leave?"

The elder missionary calculated her answer, then said, "I do. Not often, but I still do. When I first came many years ago, I nearly left on more than one occasion. But when it came right down to it, I couldn't bring myself to leave these hurting people."

Anne was shocked by the disclosure. By her intrigued expression, she pleaded with Bernice for more words of wisdom.

Bernice said, "I think those feelings are natural. When the time comes that you can bring yourself to go home, then it's probably God's time for you to go."

Returning to her work, Anne let out a surprising chuckle. "I'll go when You're ready for me to go, dear Father, and not until," she whispered.

23
Earthquake!

After a lengthy lecture from Helen, Harry was convinced to spend the hot, humid months of 1934 in the high country where his tattered body could recuperate in the cool climate. Harry and Helen rented a small bungalow near the Mount Herman School in Darjeeling where the children were enrolled.

One day just after tea, the ground shook and the walls began to stretch and separate. Harry and Helen ran outside, pulling Homer with them, only to see the earth crumbling beneath their feet. They ducked under an automobile and held onto a tire.

As soon as the rumbling came to a halt, Harry scampered down the road to locate his daughters who were visiting at the home of a friend. Extensive structural damage had occurred; several buildings lost entire walls. He later learned the school auditorium and dormitories had also suffered severe damage. Small children could be heard crying; others walked around in bewilderment, their faces and clothing smudged with dirt.

"Beatrice! Almeta! Doris! Mildred!" Harry called.

No response.

Again and again he hollered their names until he finally found Beatrice and Mildred still latched to a tree.

"Everything's okay," Harry said comfortingly, as they relinquished their grasp of the trunk and clasped onto him. "Are you all right?"

"Yes," Beatrice sighed, and Mildred bobbed her head.

"Where are your sisters?"

"Over there," Beatrice pointed. The other two girls were held up in some bushes across the yard.

Before long, Harry had all four of them holding hands and walking back to the bungalow.

Helen met the survivors at the door and caught them in her arms, silently thanking God for His protective power.

Just days after the earthquake, Harry resumed his manual labor. The school principal offered to provide the girls free tuition and give the family a patch of land if Harry oversaw the repairs to the facility. Harry began working strenuous days, hour after hour, within reach of the sun's rays. Without warning, the missionary collapsed. Three school children found him face down on the red dirt and quickly summoned a nurse.

Helen had recited another warning to him the very day that Harry agreed to undertake the maintenance work. "He's suffering from exhaustion," the doctor confirmed. "Make sure he stays down for several weeks."

Helen shook her head, certain her husband would be back to work within a few days. And that he was.

The earlier departure of Willard and Donald, who were adjusting well to American life, made the decision to send Beatrice and Almeta to school in the States easier. They would enroll in the same school Donald attended in Columbia, South Carolina. But when the two girls boarded the train in Calcutta bound for Bombay, where they would meet their chaperons, Beatrice and Almeta began to weep. Harry and Helen waved and shouted to their darlings, but in response, all the girls could do was showcase their troubled faces from the jammed window of their compartment.

"Honey, did we do the right thing in sending them away? Maybe we should wait until they're a little older," Helen suggested.

"This is the right time. They need to be with children of their own age and culture."

"But . . . but maybe we should send them next year. I can send word to Bombay to have them sent back."

Harry paused. In his heart he wanted them to stay, but he knew they could not.

Helen begged him with her eyes and partly clenched teeth.

Rather than eke out words his wife did not want to hear, Harry answered with a stern look.

Helen dropped her hands from the grip she had on his forearm and retreated to her bedroom.

Harry wanted to chase her, but he knew she needed to sort out her feelings for herself.

24
Tireless Service

In 1936, renowned missionary Robert Cummings came to Lucknow as the guest speaker of the convention of North India churches and missionaries of the Assemblies of God. Local natives and British residents, many of whom were unbelievers, converged on the large tent. One such man was a retired English army officer. He accepted Christ during the convention and approached Harry and the Reverend Cummings after one of the services.

He said, "I have sinned. Years ago I was a military supervisor over the army's supplies. Without paying for it, I took anything I wanted: clothing, furniture, anything I wanted."

Reverend Cummings said, "If you are genuinely sorry and have asked God for His forgiveness, then you have His forgiveness."

"Yes, I believe that, but I want to make restitution."

The reverend looked over at Harry for his suggestion.

Harry asked, "How much are you wanting to make restitution for?"

The man thought for a moment. "Two thousand rupees."

"Are you certain this is what you want to do? Are you prepared to pay two thousand rupees right now?"

"Yes," the man confirmed. "I have the money."

"Then follow me," Harry said.

The three men proceeded to the local post office where they purchased stamps totaling two thousand rupees. Then, in a secluded alley, Harry and the Reverend Cummings looked on as the former officer lit a match to the stamps. Restitution was served.

The man grabbed for the preachers' hands. "Thank you! Thank you for your help. Now I can face my Savior with a clean heart and without the guilt I have carried for years."

The following night, Harry was elected superintendent by the missionaries who comprised the North India District of the Assemblies of God. Amidst applause that made the tent sway, Harry walked to the podium to address his peers. Then those in attendance stood to their feet.

Motioning for them to sit, he said, "Thank you for this honor and your confidence. Most of all, it is my prayer that we will work together to see God's will accomplished. I believe God wants to use this gathering of people to reach this country with the gospel."

As he continued his acceptance speech, Helen sat in a middle row, sobbing ecstatically, yet wondering if her husband had taken on more responsibility than he could physically endure. The constituency didn't know Harry was still experiencing periods of exhaustion and shortness of breath. But they soon learned the gravity of his condition.

In 1936, a few months before Anne left to take charge of a missionary work in Lakhimpur, India, Willard returned to the mission. Harry's heart was slowing him down, so the Assemblies of God asked Willard to rejoin his father. For Harry, his eldest son's arrival was like that of a hero coming to the rescue.

When the two men exchanged stares, each met with surprise. The innocent boy Harry had sent away was now a grown man who stood with an aura of self-confidence.

The hard-working father Willard had left behind now exhibited the wear of years.

Harry walked slowly toward his son. Willard raced to his father.

Clenched in his father's limp arms, Willard said, "I missed you, Dad. It's great to see you."

"I missed you too, son. I'm thankful God has brought you back to us. You're needed here."

By his father's tone and choice of words, Willard deduced his duties would be far greater than anything he dealt with as a youth.

While attending college, Willard became engaged to Alice Haight. Her grandparents were missionaries to India, and her mother had been born there. So it was no surprise that she too felt a calling to missionary work. Alice had just completed her nurses training in England before arriving at the leper facility, so she was hailed as a welcomed addition to the missionary team.

Their wedding ceremony was held in the mission, the natives again transforming the leper home into something resembling a fairgrounds with paper and flowers of every shape and color.

As Harry prayed over the handsome couple, his voice squeaked with emotion. He was not well. For that reason, Willard had expressed concern to his mother that the emotional strain of the event might be too much for his father's failing heart.

Though she shared Willard's reservations, Helen knew Harry far too well: he was going to conduct the ceremony even if it killed him.

Harry seized a deep breath between each sentence. His speech was slow, but he managed to complete the task. He prayed, "Bless them, dear heavenly Father. Thank you for giving us such a wonderful son and giving him a beautiful wife. May they love You and serve You . . . . Amen."

Harry appeared amused as his son nervously saluted his bride.

As the recessional started, the veteran missionary made his way to a chair, the effects of his years of labor becoming all the more obvious. His heart was banging rapidly, his breathing becoming more severe; yet, from his chair, Harry could still whisper, "Dear Lord, I love you. Thank you for giving Helen and me so much to be grateful for."

Many Indian couples were not fortunate enough to choose their spouses. Marriages were arranged by relatives, sometimes at birth. Often a decision was based entirely on the size of the dowry the girl's father could afford to pay the groom's father.

Even the leper home did not escape the customs of Indian matrimony. A distant missionary wrote Harry concerning a young native Bible student who was searching for a fine Christian wife. The missionary wanted permission to send the young man to the mission to be introduced to the older girls living at the orphanage.

When the girls heard of the prince who was going to ride into the haven, they primped to look their finest, hoping they would be his Cinderella.

Harry seated the young man in his office. Beauties were ushered in one after another so the bachelor could ask questions about their cooking skills, religious beliefs, and views on raising children.

"Sahib," the young man announced, "I have chosen my wife: Asha."

"Asha?" Harry asked with a hint of surprise, for she was a plump, shy girl.

"Yes, that is who I choose."

Harry said, "No doubt she will make you very happy. Let us prepare immediately for the wedding."

Because it was taboo to travel alone with an unmarried woman, the couple was married that afternoon in the chapel with a resilient Harry performing another ceremony.

One day while supervising a crew of harvesters in the rice field, Harry was informed that four missionaries were seriously ill and needed his attention. Without explanation, he rounded up an oxcart and a few workers and sped out the gate.

He found the four men in a village twenty-two miles north on the Nepal border. Noticing that they shook incessantly and their foreheads were afire, Harry assumed they suffered from typhoid fever. Harry had the strangers carried to the oxcart, then urgently steered the team of oxen back to the leper compound.

When she heard the beating hooves and the jingle of the reins, Helen stepped onto the porch, her hands on her hips.

"Where did you run off to?" she asked, thinking this particular escape was another chapter in Harry's history of hasty departures. Helen repeated, "Where did you go?"

She had witnessed her husband's impulsive departures before. One time, when a missionary begged to be taken to his mission station to live his final days, Harry walked beside his bed for twelve miles. Another time, Harry heard about a missionary who was suffering with smallpox at a distant mission station. Despite the danger of catching the contagious illness, Harry left his duties to catch a train in Uska Bazar. While waiting at the train station, he received word the missionary had died.

Helen's disgust quickly subsided as she spotted the malnourished men.

"Hurry, we're going to need your help," Harry ordered frantically, without explaining where he had been. "We have some very sick men in the back."

Helen ran to tend to the four groaning forms.

Shaking her head, she whispered to herself, "Why did Harry have to go? Someone else could have gone. He's not strong enough."

As if hearing her complaint, Harry said, "They needed help, honey."

Rather than chastise him again, Helen sighed, "You'll never slow down, will you?"

Harry smirked.

Helen smirked back as if to say, "We'll finish this conversation later, young man."

25
More Goodbyes

Like their brothers and sisters before them, Doris and Mildred did not want to leave India in 1937. But again their parents insisted, so the family journeyed to Calcutta, a bustling city, where the girls would catch the ocean liner for America.

It was already dark when they arrived at the large ship, so Harry and Helen checked the girls on board.

"Why can't we stay with you tonight?" Doris asked.

"You'll be fine. The ship doesn't leave until tomorrow morning, so we'll be here first thing to see you off," Harry said. "We'll get a room in town and be here before you wake, okay?"

Neither Doris nor Mildred responded as he bent down and gave them an embrace. Helen's hugs were longer and just as firm.

The girls waved unenthusiastically as their parents retreated down the loading ramp.

The following morning, the Waggoners arrived to bid their girls farewell only to see instead a panoramic view of the water. The ship was no longer docked where it had been the night before.

Harry quickly approached an attendant. "Where's the ship?" he demanded.

Noticing the harshness of Harry's syllables, the boy stammered momentarily before saying, "It left during the night, sir."

"What? Why? It was supposed to leave this morning."

"I do not know."

Harry exhaled emphatically to release his anger.

Returning to where Helen was stationed, he said, "They're gone. They left during the night."

Helen threw herself into her husband's arms and wrapped herself around him. Together they cried for what seemed like an hour.

Had they known what Doris and Mildred were about to endure, they would have cried even more.

About five hours off the India coast, a torrential storm threatened to capsize the huge ship. Passengers were strapped to their beds as the vessel soared and submerged at the mercy of the wall-like waves.

Hours after the ship's crew regained control of the wheel, the girls' stomachs were still tumbling. To avoid the apex of the storm, the captain detoured to San Francisco. From there the girls boarded a train destined for Springfield, Missouri, where they met Donald. He chauffeured them to school in South Carolina.

Although anxious to see their first American tiger running across a field and huge snake slithering onto a dirt path, the girls marveled at the spacious homes, plush automobiles, and the monstrous office complexes.

Several years later, Homer prepared himself for the voyage to the States to attend school. He said goodbye to his orphan pal, Lawrence, then threw his suitcase into the rear seat of the Ford. As the vehicle bounced toward Uska Bazar, it never occurred to him that he would never see the mission again.

"Homer," Harry said, "you know we've been having it hard financially. Do you have any money you could spare to get me home?"

Homer's drooping eyes drifted toward his pocket as a dollar bill materialized. "This is all I have."

"May I have it? I hate to say this, but I need it more than you do."

The twelve-year-old handed over the currency, embraced his parents, and boarded the train.

With the last of his children departed, Harry fought to fill the void with prayers. "Protect them. Be the parents we cannot be. Provide for them, dear Jesus."

Despite his faith in God and repetitive prayers, the myriad of memories of his children kept materializing in his thoughts. He missed them terribly, and there was nothing he could do to relieve the pain.

Waiting for Harry when he returned to the leper home was Munshi, a young man who had been hired sometime earlier to help oversee the orphanage.

"Sahib, sir, I would like to discuss with you the furthering of my education."

"Okay," Harry said.

"I would like to take my wife and complete my studies of the Bible in the United States."

"That is very expensive, Munshi. And we do not have the funds to help you."

"This I know, but Miss Dutton said she may know someone who could help me."

Harry was silent for a moment. "I cannot tell you what to do, but I must be honest with you and say that I do not think highly of the idea."

A defiant, scornful expression crossed Munshi's face. "Why? Don't you want me to learn more about the Bible?"

"Most certainly I do. I want what's best for you and for the orphans who lean on you."

"Yohan is here. He is capable. Besides, sometimes one must be concerned with himself and his future. I'm sorry,

Sahib, but I will be leaving as soon as I have raised the support I need."

Harry slowly turned away from his friend, muzzling what would have been angry words.

26
Separation

News of the bombing of Pearl Harbor swept around the globe, and it was obvious that World War II was escalating. German forces advanced toward Egypt. Japanese troops moved into Singapore and Burma. And factions within India performed acts of sabotage. British officials feared the battlefield might extend farther into India. By the hour, mission workers huddled around a small battery-powered radio to hear the latest war news.

On a regrettable morning, a British magistrate, one who had been thoughtful of Harry's social work, conveyed a troubling request to the missionary. Britain's Parliament recommended that women and children of English descent return to their homelands until the fighting curtailed. A letter from the American embassy made a similar request, claiming the United States government could not offer adequate protection to its citizens in India. Although Harry wanted to deny the petition, he realized it was a necessary precaution.

Not even a cool afternoon could make the departure of Helen and some of the other female workers easier for Harry.

Harry tried to reason why God would separate him from his wife. At a time when he was so fatigued, he asked, why would God allow workers to leave? The many hours of pondering served only to make him more lonely and distressed. He feared he would not survive without Helen by his side to console him after wearisome days.

On his knees early one morning, while praying for his wife, Harry felt the presence of God like he hadn't since her departure. These words burst into his thoughts: "Rest in the knowledge that I am God. I have everything under control."

The missionary rose to his feet as though he had met God face to face. The foreboding days ahead—the loneliness, workload, and health problems—were indeed worthy foes. But he said to Willard later that day, "Son, God is in control and He will have His way. He's not going to let us down. We merely have to do His will."

Willard shook his head in support.

But Harry knew the agony of loneliness could not be swept away by his own words. Realizing only God could soothe his aching heart, he prayed by the hour for divine comfort.

Because some civilian-carrying ships had been sunk by enemy torpedoes, Harry was grateful to learn that Helen had landed safely. She took up residence in Ohio where Mildred was living. Although she was comfortable and protected, Helen found relief from the despairing months of separation in reading the Bible and Harry's letters. Helen clung to his correspondence, reading the sheaves of paper over and over again.

Shortly after some of the women had vacated the country, Munshi and his wife returned to work in the leper home. They had completed their studies in the States, and their return was timely and appreciated. But Harry recognized some subtle changes in his friend's attitude—exactly why he objected to him going abroad in the first place.

While in school, Munshi had raised missionary funds from churches and wealthy Christians. He no longer viewed himself as a subordinate to Harry, but as a missionary in his own right just waiting for his opportunity to wrestle the ministry from his "former" employer. He wore nice clothing, his hair was well-groomed, and he considered himself better than the average native.

Harry could not deny his love for Munshi, and during this period of a depleted work force, he knew he needed the Indian's assistance. The situation was compounded in 1944 when failing health forced Willard to leave the country. Malaria and typhoid had stolen his strength, and he had to make a hasty retreat to America.

With Willard's departure, it was fortunate that Helen could return to Harry's side after twelve months of separation. When she stepped off the train, her husband caught her in his arms like a groom carrying his bride across a threshold.

In the months that followed, the senior missionaries tried to manage the compound, but Harry's health began to fade quickly under the pressure of lengthy days and improper nourishment. Finally, with a promise from missionaries in the surrounding stations to oversee the leper home and keep a close watch on Munshi, Harry agreed to return to the States for a period of recuperation in 1946. Once his health improved, the missionaries agreed, he would be able to resume his ministry at the mission.

The Waggoners longed to see their children, but Harry especially abhorred the idea of leaving his home among the lepers for a paradise of hot showers, ice cubes, and restaurants. The lepers begged them to stay, partly because they did not trust Munshi, but mostly because they would miss their spiritual shepherds.

Harry locked himself in his room one afternoon. He paced from wall to wall and began speaking audibly to

God. "I have given my life to this place. And You know I don't want to leave. Somehow, for some reason, I feel like You are opening the door for me to leave for a while. I don't understand. There is so much to do here, and yet we need to see our kids. I need to regain my strength. Help me to be obedient. Are You telling us to leave, or are You wanting to heal me so we can continue here? I need to hear Your voice, to know Your will."

Several days later, on a Monday afternoon fit for an afternoon stroll, the aging couple stepped into the front seat of the old Ford. Harry and Helen were showered with flowers and homemade gifts as the vehicle poked toward the mission gate. Harry felt like a king deserting his followers. Despite the emptiness and despair they felt, the Waggoners waved and smiled at the crowd. They wanted to proclaim they would return in just a few months, but, realistically, they knew they could be certain of nothing—not even Munshi's loyalty.

27
Treasured Moments

As the huge ocean liner drifted to the dock in New York City in 1946, Harry felt like a tourist visiting a foreign land for the first time. This no longer felt like home. It wasn't home.

Even the train ride to Wisconsin—passing through one attractive town after another—could not make this occasion seem like the festive homecoming it should have been. For Harry, the lone allurement of American soil was the hope of seeing his children. While resting in a cottage on Spencer Lake in Wisconsin, Harry relished time spent with his children as they came to welcome him home.

Those were precious times of laughter and reflection; the visits gave Harry an opportunity to get reacquainted with the faces he had nearly forgotten.

Soon after Harry's health permitted, he began accepting speaking engagements. The veteran missionary had little money and no transportation, so Donald, who was pastoring in Wisconsin, resigned his position to travel with his father for three months.

Helen stayed at home while the father and son team ministered in small and large churches alike. The duo spent their days on the road joyfully reminiscing and discussing the future of the work in India.

One night following a service, Helen phoned her husband. She said, "Have you heard? Britain has given India home rule and much of the property is reverting to native ownership."

Harry was deathly silent.

"Did you hear what I said?"

"Yes," he answered after another pause.

"Is there anything we can do?"

"To be honest with you, I don't know."

Ultimately, Harry hoped the natives would run the mission compound, but he had strong reservations about Munshi's self-centered leadership. He questioned whether his one-time associate really cared for the lepers. He wondered how the lepers, sensing Munshi's greed, would respond to him.

Harry's attempts to correspond with his substitute were unsuccessful. He feared his influence over the mission was being eroded.

His instincts were right.

Munshi had bribed a judge to rule Harry had deeded the property to him before leaving the country. In the court's view, Harry no longer held ownership of the land. It belonged to Munshi. Because of the ruling, the neighboring mission stations no longer had authority to interfere with the leper home.

Perhaps it was the lure of India or the fear of Munshi that expedited Harry's return to better health. Nevertheless, he knew he was too late. Munshi had successfully engineered his scheme. Harry concluded he could not return to the mission without risking personal harm because Munshi wielded much influence in the community. He feared his life work had been in vain and that God was disappointed with him. He lingered in his room for days, praying that

God would perform a miracle; that God would judge Munshi harshly if he mistreated the lepers.

Harry was virtually penniless and he had no home. And he had too much self-respect to live off his children.

It was during this period of inner turmoil that a pastor in Winnipeg invited the Waggoners to take up residence in their church-owned apartment. With limited options before them, Harry and Helen accepted the offer, all the while dreaming of returning to the homeland, yet knowing full well Harry was not fit for a lengthy fight.

By 1948, however, he was fit to assume a pastorate in Crosby, North Dakota. The seventy-five member congregation was a far cry from his congregation at the mission, but it proved to be a rewarding experience. Unfortunately, the frigid snowstorms eventually forced the Waggoners to leave; the weather was so unlike the climate to which they had grown accustomed in India.

Harry and Helen moved to Caldwell, Idaho, where Willard was working as a photographer and part-time radio announcer. Before long, Harry also joined the work force. It was one of the proudest days of his life when he walked through their screen door having just been employed by the Glen Evens Fish and Fly Factory. He began working as an assembler and, gradually, regained his familiar grin. He became active in a local church and spent his free time gardening, reading, and writing words of encouragement to other ministers. As Helen put it, God had decided to give Harry "an extended sabbatical" to make up for lost time with his family.

Late one October, Harry, Willard, and Don all went hunting. Bagging two nice bucks was exciting, but the times around the campfire each evening were the highlights of the trip.

After throwing kindling into the fire, Willard and Donald sat mesmerized by the flame.

Harry said, "I just wish we had done more of this when you were young."

"We understood, Dad," Donald said. "You were like a father to so many. You had a lot of responsibility."

"Don't worry. I think we turned out all right, don't you?" Willard added.

Harry grinned and said, "You did at that. I'm real proud of each one of you. God had to teach you some things, and you had to learn some lessons on your own because I was too busy doing other things. I regret that."

Willard and Donald sensed their father was trying to proffer an apology. As youngsters, they resented his busy schedule at times. They wanted to spend more time with him; still, they never doubted his genuine love for his children.

In response to his apology, the sons echoed one another, saying, "I love you, Dad." To themselves they were only wishing they had all the time in the world to be together, "to make up for lost time."

28
Farewell to a Hero

Spring 1956. Willard rushed to a pay phone to call his brothers and sisters. Harry had suffered an attack of some kind and was in the hospital in Caldwell. Willard, Helen, and Katie waited for the doctor's diagnosis in a hallway where nurses chattered in small circles and doctors, clinging onto clipboards, dashed from room to room.

A white-coated doctor suddenly appeared at Helen's side. "Mrs. Waggoner, your husband has suffered a heart attack. He's out of immediate danger, but he'll have to stay here for a while so we can do more tests."

"When can we see him?" Willard asked.

"He should be awake in several hours."

Helen heard the doctor, but she could not utter a response. The thought of losing Harry had entered her mind before, but the reality of it was terrifying.

Eleven days later Harry returned home. Mildred and Donald drove immediately to Idaho to lend their support. When they arrived they found their father solemn and dejected. His demeanor did not change for days. Nothing seemed to raise his spirits. All he could think about was India and the reality that he might never return. He did not want to talk, nor offer enchanting smiles. He wanted to be left to himself.

The day before she was to leave, Mildred began playing the organ, and, astonishingly, from his prone position on the couch, Harry began whistling the melody of "Be still my soul, the Lord is on my side." Tears welled up in his eyes, and he whispered, "Thank You, God." For the children and Helen, it was the first sign of hope that he would fully recover.

In time, the "warrior" would return to his job at the factory and resume his leadership role in the local church. Those who knew him well said he was "as good as new—the old Harry."

In celebration of the Waggoners' fiftieth wedding anniversary, a family reunion was held in the summer of 1962. The picnic atmosphere under the warm sun, with children playing games and running races, reminded Harry of the holidays at the leper home. Everyone was reveling in the festivity. Even their two-year-old granddaughter Doree was laughing and pulling on Harry's arms. Everything seemed to be so perfect.

To the dismay of Beatrice and Doris, they found their mother alone crying in their automobile.

Before the daughters could inquire, Helen sighed, "I'm crying because this is probably the last time we're all going to be together. I just don't want it to end."

"Mom, you don't know that," Beatrice said, Doris nodding in agreement.

Helen shook her head. "Your father is not very well. He's not going to be with us much longer."

The two daughters glanced at each other then at their mother, wondering if she knew something they didn't.

Helen continued, "I've felt his heart racing so fast at night. Sometimes I can't even sleep because of it."

"Has he been going to the doctor?" Doris asked.

"Yes, but there's only so much they can do," she said, pausing to wipe her eyes. "I guess I shouldn't be ruining your day like this, but I can't help it."

"We love you, Mom," Beatrice said, squeezing her shoulder.

"Always," Doris added.

Wednesday, March 6, 1963. Willard spotted his father shuffling up the sidewalk on his way home. He enjoyed his leisurely walks into town and back. Pulling up beside him, Willard rolled down the window. "You want a ride, Dad?"

Harry slid in beside his son, breathing heavily.

"Are you okay?" Willard inquired.

Within seconds, Harry grabbed his chest and passed out.

Willard knew what was happening and sped to the nearest hospital. Once Harry was in the care of physicians, Willard raced back to collect his mother. Sitting in the waiting room, Helen was too panicked at first to shed a tear. She tried to maintain a glimmer of courage before releasing an awful shrill. Tears coursed down the wrinkles in her face. The doctor had told them several years earlier that one more heart attack would be his last. The inevitable was beginning to sink in. Without God's intervention, today Harry would meet his Maker.

Willard let his mother hide in his arms.

Wiping their tears, mother and son could see the doctor coming, his footsteps echoing down the long hospital corridor.

Softly, the doctor said, "I'm sorry, Mrs. Waggoner, but there's nothing more we can do. He's in and out of consciousness, but he may go at any time. I'm sorry."

Helen whimpered, latched onto Willard's arm for support, and proceeded to her husband's room.

"Harry, can you hear me?" she said, leaning over his bed to look him in the eye.

He nodded his head, though his eyes were filled with fluid and only partly open.

Willard turned his head momentarily to hide his tears. Harry's eyes were already beginning to close. Willard glanced up. Only Harry's eyelids were visible.

Several days later, with his wife and eldest son by his bedside, with one last gasp, Harry's chin dropped against his sternum. The monitor and alarm signaled the end of a hero's life.

Helen grabbed Harry's hand and held it until it was time to leave the room.

The funeral was a tribute to a man who had given his seventy-one years and made countless sacrifices so others could be exposed to the love of Jesus Christ. It was a tribute to a legacy he had left for his children, grandchildren, great-grandchildren, and future missionaries.

Those who attended the funeral walked away certain of one thought: when Harry Waggoner walked through the Pearly Gates, there was a long line of lepers there to greet him—there to show off their unblemished hands, feet, and faces—there to say thank you for showing them the way to eternal life through Jesus Christ. "Piyare Sahibjee, A-yea!" they shouted triumphantly, meaning, "Beloved Sahib, Welcome."

Epilogue

Helen Waggoner lived out her remaining days in Ohio with her daughter Mildred before dying in 1980 at the age of eighty-nine.

Donald returned to India and the site of the leper home in 1974. There he found twenty-five lepers, Yohan, and Munshi—though just a morsel of his former self.

"Know who that is?" Yohan asked.

"No," Donald answered.

"That's Munshi."

Donald stared in disbelief. Munshi was unshaven, barefoot, his hair unkempt, and his dhoti was hanging out. He had lost his wife and family and become a drunkard.

Donald said to Yohan, "He certainly has suffered the consequences of his greed and ungodliness, hasn't he?"

The facilities were overgrown with weeds, and the buildings were in disrepair.

It was a heart-wrenching scene for Harry's son to witness. For an instant, he wished he had never returned. What was once such a God-honoring facility was now dilapidated. Donald responded to the eyesore the same way his father would have: he wept.

Nevertheless, Donald was comforted to learn that Yohan was still caring for the lepers. He was a servant to the hurting and diseased of the region. God had raised up Yohan so the work would not die, nor would the memory of Harry Waggoner. Unbeknownst to the Waggoner children, this short, thin man—who was raised in this mission—had followed in Harry's footsteps. As Harry had prophesied years earlier, Yohan was special; God *had* sent him to the mission for a reason.

More than fifteen years after Donald's return to the compound, Willard paid his own visit. And while he was distressed with the facility's condition, he was grateful to learn the lepers and natives were still reciting the legendary stories Yohan and others had told them. They spoke freely of a loving white man who was sent to them by a loving God many years ago. They told stories of his compassion and sacrifice. They spoke of his generosity.

Then, with tears in their eyes and a smile on their faces, they confessed that they still dream of the day that this missionary or someone like him will return.

About the Authors

Hal Donaldson is a journalism graduate of San Jose State University. He served as editor of *On Magazine* and taught at Bethany College. He is president of ChurchCare Network, an organization that sends ministries—at no cost—to smaller churches. He has authored numerous books, including *Where is the Lost Ark?*, *One Man's Compassion*, *Treasures in Heaven*, and *Ungagging the Church*.

Kenneth M. Dobson is the president of Onward Books, Inc. He left a successful business career to enter full-time ministry many years ago. He received his B.A. in Biblical Literature from Northwest College and his M.A. in Church Leadership from Southern California College. He formerly served with Mark and Huldah Buntain in Calcutta, India, before accepting the pastorate of First Assembly of God in Paramount, California. Reverend Dobson also actively serves on the board of directors of several non-profit organizations.